ORDERING YOUR
PRIVATE WORLD

BY THE SAME AUTHOR

Forging a Real-World Faith

Rebuilding Your Broken World

Restoring Your Spiritual Passion

When Men Think Private Thoughts

The Life God Blesses

Mid-Course Correction

A Resilient Life

ORDERING YOUR PRIVATE WORLD

by

Gordon MacDonald

Highland Books

Cover design: Inspiration-by-Design, Worthing
ISBN: 1 897913 67 2

Printed in Great Britain for HIGHLAND BOOKS
Two High Pines, Knoll Road
GODALMING, Surrey GU7 2EP
by Bookmarque Ltd

Contents

Foreword by Selwyn Hughes - - - - - - - - - 7

Preface: The Day I Hit the Wall - - - - - - 9

1.   The Sinkhole Syndrome - - - - - 21

2.   A View from the Bridge - - - - - - 31

Sector one : motivation »   »   »   »   »   39

3.   Caught in a Golden Cage - - - - - 41

4.   The Tragic Tale of a Successful Bum - - 61

5.   Living as a Called Person - - - - - 71

Sector two: use of time »   »   »   »   »   89

6.   Has Anyone Seen My Time? I've Misplaced It! 91

7.   Recapturing My Time - - - - - - 103

Sector three: wisdom and knowledge »   »   »   119

8.   The Better Man Lost - - - - - - 121

9.   The Sadness of a Book Never Read - - - 137

Sector four: spiritual strength »   »   »   »   155

10.   Order in the Garden - - - - - - 157

11.   No Outer Props Necessary - - - - - 169

12.   Everything Has to Be Entered - - - - 187

13.   Seeing Through Heaven's Eyes - - - - 195

Sector five: restoration »   »   »   »   »   213

14.   Rest Beyond Leisure - - - - - - 215

Epilogue: The Spinning Wheel - - - - - - 235

Study guide: »   »   »   »   »   »   241

Notes: - - - - - - - - - - - 281

To the Grace Chapel family of Lexington,
Massachussetts, my brothers and sisters,
my co-workers, my friends:

Much of what this book is about,
I learned from you.

Foreword by Selwyn Hughes

Occasionally a book appears in print that speaks so expertly to basic human needs that one is set on fire to absorb it. This is such a book.

My attention was first drawn to it by a missionary from the Far East who, when passing through the United States on the way home to England, purchased a copy and found it to be 'compelling and fascinating reading'. She loaned me her copy for a few hours and as I skimmed through its pages I soon realised that this was material that deserved to be constantly at hand on my bookshelf.

In *Ordering Your Private World* Gordon MacDonald not only paints a glorious picture of what life can be like when our inner world is ordered but he shows us the steps we need to take in order to achieve it. His thesis is simple but powerful. How can our outer world be orderly if our inner world is not? How indeed?

A psychiatrist told me some years ago that people don't so much break down as 'fall to pieces'. Unless the pieces are held together by some inner cement then life soon becomes strained, and hence drained. So many of us need to see that in order to live effectively it is not so much the outer circumstances that have to be ordered, but our *inner-stances*. When things are right on the inside — in our private world — then, and only then, can we face the past, present and future with confidence and certainty.

Gordon MacDonald has done the Christian Church a tremendous service with this book. I warmly commend it.

Selwyn Hughes

The Day I Hit the Wall

ONE SATURDAY MORNING IN MY THIRTIETH YEAR, AN event occurred that changed my life.

I was a young pastor in a sizeable church, and I had accumulated several weeks of busyness (I mean *really* busy!) in my work. Now, there is a busyness that reflects a plan of activity, a pattern of priorities, and a sense of purposefulness. It is a good and satisfying busyness through which one grows and increases competence.

But there is also a busyness (a destructive busyness, actually) that reflects a chaotic way of life – a way of doing in which one is simply responding to the next thing in the day. *The next thing!* It makes no difference whether or not it has significance; it's just the next thing, and one does it because it's there to do.

In that thirtieth year I was swept along in that second kind of busyness much like someone being swept along in the rapids of a raging river. Out of control. Fearful of capsizing. Feeling quite unprotected.

Day after day I had risen before the sun, and night after night I had fallen into bed long past the time when TV used to sign off. The hours of each day had been filled with business meetings, people with problems, speeches and talks that came one after another, and – added to all of this – the normal administrative details that dog anyone who is in charge of an organization.

But that wasn't all. During that time there had been the deaths of two homeless men in our community. I had supervised the arrangements for their burials. The utter senselessness of their lives and the sadness of their lonely deaths had touched me deeply and sent me into a dark, cloudy mood.

Oh, there was also a book that everyone said I should be reading. I'd purchased it and was reading snippets of it now and then. Its author seemed to attack everything I believed in and did it in such a convincing way that I felt the foundations of my entire belief system threatened. I couldn't get the book out of my thoughts.

All of it – the incessant work, that inky mood, those destabilizing thoughts – had done nothing but drain me: spiritually, emotionally, intellectually, and physically. Drained is certainly the operative word, and it was a surprising sensation because, like most young adults, I assumed that energy and vitality were boundless and inexhaustible. I'm embarrassed to admit that I was unconsciously convinced that one could live at this furious pace forever and do it without any serious consequences.

And now, as I said at the beginning, it was Saturday, and I sat at our breakfast table trying to act in a sociable way toward my young family yet, all the while, preoccupied with the stuff that lay ahead of me in the next hours. At the top of my mental pile were the events of Sunday, twenty-four hours away, when I would have to stand before audiences on three separate occasions and give presentations for which, so far, I had done no preparation.

It was at that moment that my wife, Gail, spoke and said something that was both true and provocative. "You've not spent much time with the children lately," she observed quietly.

And I began to cry. Not a few tears and not for a short while. I cried for at least four hours . . . great, wrenching sobs that came from near, as best I can figure, the bottomless pit of my soul.

Gail, showing remarkable wisdom, asked a neighbour to watch our two children, and then held me in her arms while I blubbered my way through the morning. She was sensitive enough to know that I did not need someone to preach at me or offer a "suck-it-up" speech. She simply shared the cathartic moments with me and assured me of her (and God's) love.

I remember the morning in considerable detail. It was as though my inner being was like a basement filled with floodwaters. But this was raw emotion and whatever was behind it. And like a flooded basement, it needed to be pumped out. Thus the wash of tears.

There were times on that Saturday morning when I thought I might be losing my mind. Was this what it was like to "crack up," as some people put it? I was used to being in control, but now I was not. I was accustomed to being strong for everyone else, but now I was the weak one. What was happening? And why had no one ever warned me (at least in ways that I could understand) that there could be moments like this?

As a lecturer and writer, I have often told the story of that Saturday morning to men and women in leadership positions, and I have been careful (because I possess all the ego traits of men who do not like to bring attention to their tears) to tell them that this morning of crying had never happened before, nor has it happened since. But it certainly did that day, and I had no choice but to allow the day's schedule to be killed and look to what had gone wrong inside me at soul-level.

Many times I have looked back wondering what I was crying for that day. Perhaps it was some of the wounds and sorrows that had been handed down from father to son from previous generations. Then again, perhaps I was weeping for my own sadnesses, the ones I had lived through as a boy and never brought to resolution. What about the possibility that I was simply reflecting weeks and weeks of stressful life in which there had been no pause and no inner, spiritual maintenance? How about the chance that it was all of these possibilities?

That Saturday was the day I learned, the hard and frightening way, that I could not go on living the way I was living and expect to be a spiritual leader (or any other kind of leader) of people. I often refer to that morning as the day I hit the wall.

I had always wanted to be a pastor. My father had been one, and my grandfather, for all practical purposes, had been one. The call to pastoral life was in my blood, you could say, and with great anticipation I pointed in that direction throughout my younger years. Even as a young boy I could see myself someday in the pulpit. When a teenager, even when I lived in a bit of spiritual defiance, I knew there would come a moment when I would capitulate to the call of God and become what he had made me to be: a pastor, a spiritual shepherd to people.

My father, an inveterate teacher, had taught me almost everything there was to know about how to lead a church. Words had come easily to me from the earliest days. So had social skills. I knew how to engage with people, think quickly on my feet, see issues and problems from the biggest possible perspective. By nature I was an idea man, a visionary of sorts, and I possessed an ability to persuade people to follow.

You call all of these things, or at least I do, natural gifts or talents. They come in the course of life to some people through our temperaments, our life experiences, and the influence of family and close friends. To a considerable extent, they were almost all the natural gifts I needed to get a very fast start in pastoral ministry.

When I use the term fast start I am referring to those things that might (but shouldn't) dazzle a young, ambitious, impressionable man or woman of any vocation. Fast start fits with the vocabulary of perceived success: large numbers, big bucks, sudden victories, quick recognition, and meeting "important" people – things which I see as rather insignificant today but in times past was tempted to take rather seriously.

This was what fast start meant for me. A midwestern congregation of several hundred people had called me right out of seminary at the age of twenty-eight to be their pastor. And in the first couple of years almost everything I did turned out right. Well, not everything. But it seemed like that.

In addition to the natural giftedness I've mentioned, there were some other very practical reasons why this fast start happened. For example, I had a remarkably mature and insightful wife who put every bit of muscle (spiritual and otherwise) she had into my ministry and saved me from a thousand errors of judgement. Then, too, my predecessor had made some serious leadership mistakes, and that meant that almost everything I did, by contrast, the congregation viewed with favour and affection.

Humanly speaking, the future looked extremely bright, and even those who had tracked my life during my school days and had sometimes worried about whether I would amount to anything were beginning to think that I might be on to something special in the future. If ministry was all about natural talent, timely opportunities, and great assistance from those who loved you, I was on my way. Natural gifts. We all have them, I suppose, some of us having more than others.

They can carry young men and women for a long distance. They certainly carried me.

Natural gifts such as personal charisma, mental brightness, emotional strength, and organizational ability can impress and motivate people for a long time. Sometimes they can be mistaken for spiritual vitality and depth. Sadly, we do not have a Christian culture today that easily discriminates between a person of spiritual depth and a person of raw talent. Like the wheat and the tares of Jesus' parable, they can be difficult to distinguish. The result is that more than a few people can be fooled into thinking they are being influenced by a spiritual giant when in fact they are being manipulated by a dwarf.

We must always be aware that there are leaders who can build great organizations (including churches) on natural gifts. Say the right words, be smart enough to do the right things, be insightful enough to connect with the right people, and one can go a long way before anyone ever discovers that the inner life is close to empty.

And that's exactly where I was that Saturday morning. A young man with a fairly empty soul, rich in natural gifts but impoverished when it came to an inner space, from which there might flow a wellspring of wisdom, spiritual power, and Christian depth.

When I had exhausted myself of my tears, I spent the remainder of the day trying to squeeze meaning out of what had happened. What was the message of the flood of tears? What was it saying about the pace and direction of my life and work? Was it a warning, an instruction, a picture of unpleasant consequences yet to come?

Let me offer the most important insight that came from the day.

For the past two to three years I had been aware of my fast start in the ministry. I had also been aware that most

– not all – of the men (in those days it was all men) who had graduated with me had gone on to assignments that were not as attractive as mine. In some sense many of them had not enjoyed the advantages that had come to me: a teaching father, natural giftedness, good connections. The result: They had to work harder, discipline themselves more carefully, and develop an inner depth that I had not found necessary to worry about.

But – and here was the kicker – it became alarmingly clear to me that day that it might not always be this way. Rather, I began to intuit that there would be a change in the years to come.

Those who brought their lives into discipline or (and this is a favourite word of mine) intentionality would, more than likely, go on to long-term lives of fruitfulness, and their best years would be in the last half of their lives when discipline and depth paid off. And those like me, who relied heavily upon our natural giftedness, would reach some high point early in our lives and, more than likely, trail off into averageness for the last half of our days on earth. Of the former it would be said, "He [she] is a person of rich spiritual quality." Of me, given where I was, it would more likely be said, "Well, he certainly was a flash in the pan."

What an innocuous way to live out one's days – a displeasure to God and certainly a regrettable muddle for oneself. The thought that this might become my life scenario was intolerable. And it was that insight and that sense of revulsion that made that Saturday into a day that changed my life.

By the end of that day you could say that I had gone through something of a conversion experience. I would deliberately reorder my life, I determined, and I would do my best to jump the track from a life and work based on natural giftedness to one built on discipline and intentionality. Or to put it in terms in keeping with the title of this book, I determined to *order my private world.*

In the hours that followed, I tried as best as I could to acknowledge to God my regret that I had misinterpreted the conduct of my life and the use of my natural gifts. I wanted him to know that I desired to change and that if He would intervene in my spiritual journey and acquaint me with some new processes of discipline, I would listen as best as I could. What I was actually seeking – put in the biggest possible terms – was a renovation of my life.

Please don't entertain the notion that everything instantly changed. It didn't. I had lots of hard work to do. In fact it would take years of hard work. I say "hard work" because the task of renovating, or reordering, one's private and public world is no small challenge. And the job never quite gets done. I have now come to understand that there are issues that I will probably take to my grave.

If there were a first step for me in my life-renovation process, it began with a simple, spiral-bound notebook that I came to call a journal. I'd read about journals from time to time, how many of the great saints had kept them and passed on to later generations the stories of their inner and outer lives. And I'd taken note that some of the modern writers whom I admire had kept journals for many years.

And so it occurred to me that there might be a secret here. And I think I was right, for the journal caused me to begin a lively and meaningful dialogue with myself. Feelings, questions, conclusions, and mysteries could all be put into words no matter how clumsy they were. Events and their larger meanings could be recorded for later recollection. And prayers and observations from the Scriptures and spiritual classics could be written out so that they were not lost nor forgotten.

That night I made my first entry into my new journal. I told the story of the early-morning hours and their tears. I talked about what it felt like to come face to face with my clogged-up soul. And I made some wild promises (one tends to do this in moments like those): that I would make entries into my journal every day, that I would stop from my labours each day and take stock of where I was and where I was going. Finally, I declared that I was going to bring my life under control, into order. I was, for sure, never going to go through a morning like that again.

These declarations and others were not easy to fulfill. I am not by nature an organized person. I do not pick up things automatically. I do not finish things before I start something else. I am not good with details. I can easily forget things I've promised to do. And I can get easily distracted. I am a daydreamer (having a very rich imagination); I can be very playful; and I can fall effortlessly into the trap of trying to please everybody. As you can imagine, there was a lot that needed renovating here.

Build an orderly life with raw material like that! But that was exactly what I had to do.

More than once, people who have read an earlier version of *Ordering Your Private World* have come up to me and said, "It must be nice to organize your life so naturally." And they are always startled when I say to them, "OPW [that's what we call it in our family] was not written by a naturally ordered man; it was written by a naturally *disordered* man who had to get his life in line if he was ever to amount to anything."

Most of the time they are encouraged by those words.

I must not conclude this introduction without emphasizing one indispensable principle. The order of my private world is an inside-out matter, not an outside-in matter. We are all too tempted to buy gadgets (organizer programs for our computers, Palm Pilots, cell phones, and BlackBerries, to name a few) with the hopes that they will bring tidiness of life. But it doesn't work that way. Forget the gadgets and start with the interior, the private world.

The order we seek begins with a thorough scouring of the inside of life. With tough questions that it may take others to help us answer. With a confronting of beliefs and principles that are toxic and destructive. With a listening to the voice of God who has better things for us.

Today I look back upon that Saturday in the thirtieth year of life – the day I hit the wall – as one of the most important days of my life journey. That was the day the warning sirens sounded, the day I saw all too clearly where I was headed if something did not change in my private world. It was the day I started the search for inner (and a resulting outer) orderliness. A process that continues until this day.

MEMO TO THE DISORGANIZED

If my private world is in order, it will be because I am convinced that the inner world of the spiritual must govern the outer world of activity.

ONE

The Sinkhole Syndrome

THE RESIDENTS OF A FLORIDA APARTMENT BUILDING awoke to a terrifying sight outside their windows. The ground beneath the street in front of their building had literally collapsed, creating a massive depression that Floridians call a sinkhole. Tumbling into the ever-deepening pit were automobiles, pavement, sidewalks, and lawn furniture. The building itself would obviously be the next to go.

Sinkholes occur, scientists say, when underground streams drain away during seasons of drought, causing the ground at the surface to lose its underlying support. Suddenly everything simply caves in, leaving people with a frightening suspicion that nothing – not even the earth beneath their feet – is trustworthy.

There are many people whose lives are like one of Florida's sinkholes. It is likely that at one time or another many of us have perceived ourselves to be on the verge of a sinkhole-like cave-in. In the feelings of numbing fatigue, a taste of apparent failure, or the bitter experience of disillusionment about goals or purposes, we may have sensed something within us about to give way. We feel we are just a moment from a collapse that will threaten to sweep our entire world into a bottomless pit. Sometimes there seems to be little that can be done to prevent such a collapse. What is wrong?

If we think about it for very long, we may discover the existence of an inner space – our private world – about which we were formerly ignorant. I hope it will become apparent that, if neglected, this private world will not sustain the weight of events and stresses that press upon us.

Some people are surprised and disturbed when they make such a self-discovery. They suddenly realize that they have spent the majority of their time and energy establishing life on the visible level, at the surface. They have accumulated a host of good and perhaps even excellent assets such as academic degrees, work experience, key relationships, and physical strength or beauty.

There is nothing wrong with all of that. But often it is discovered almost too late that the private world of the person is in a state of disorderliness or weakness. And when that is true, there is always potential for the sinkhole syndrome.

We must come to see ourselves as living in two very different worlds. Our outer, or public, world is easier to deal with. It is much more measurable, visible, and expandable. Our outer world consists of work, play, possessions, and a host of acquaintances that make up a social network. It is the part of our existence easiest to evaluate in terms of success, popularity, wealth, and beauty. But our inner world is more spiritual in nature. Here is a centre in which choices and values can be determined, where solitude and reflection might be pursued. It is a place for conducting worship and confession, a spot where the moral and spiritual pollution of the times need not penetrate.

The majority of us have been taught to manage our public worlds well. Of course, there will always be the undependable worker, the poorly organized homemaker, and the person whose social capacities are so immature that he becomes a drain on everyone around him. But most of us have learned to take orders, make schedules, and give directions. We know which systems best suit us in terms of work and relationship. We choose proper forms of leisure and pleasure. We have the ability to choose friends and make those relationships work well.

Our public worlds are filled with a seeming infinity of demands upon our time, our loyalties, our money, and our energies. And because these public worlds of ours are so visible, so real, we have to struggle to ignore all their seductions and demands. They scream for our attention and action.

But there is this private world in every one of us. A world that may be as infinite in size as we perceive our public worlds to be. But often the private world – like the depths of the ocean – remains unexplored, full of surprises, ambushes, emotions, and dreams.

In a past season of the popular television series *Survivor*, one of the finalists, Jerry, talked about the pressures she faced as she tried to avoid getting voted off the island. When asked if she had surprised herself in her drive to win the million-dollar prize, she said, "Honestly? I had no idea that this was going to be as tough as it is. I have woken up in the morning and gone through an entire day wondering who I am. Things come out of my mouth in frustration and hunger and . . . stress that, after they come out, I want to suck them back in, because it's not the same thing I would normally say or [do] . . . so, yeah, I've surprised myself in a lot of ways."

Although Jerry describes life in a contrived (made-for-TV) world, she speaks like a fast-tracker. As life heats up, she seems amazed to discover traits of personal character that she really didn't want to own.

In a real world similar to Jerry's, there is a temptation to ignore the existence of our private world because it does not shout quite so loudly when neglected. It can be effectively short-changed for large periods of time before it gives way to a sinkhole-like cave-in.

Oscar Wilde, author and playwright, was one who paid scant attention to his private world. William Barclay quotes Wilde's confession:

> The gods had given me almost everything. But I let myself be lured into long spells of senseless and sensual ease . . . Tired of being on the heights, I deliberately went to the depths in search for new sensation. What the paradox was to me in the sphere of thought, perversity became to me in the sphere of passion. I grew careless of the lives of others. I took pleasure where it pleased me, and passed on. I forgot that every little action of the common day makes or unmakes character, and that therefore what one has done in the secret chamber, one has some day to cry aloud from the house-top. I ceased to be lord over myself. I was no longer the captain of my soul, and did not know it. I allowed pleasure to dominate me. I ended in horrible disgrace.[1]

When Wilde wrote, "I was no longer the captain of my soul," he described a person whose inner world was in shambles, whose life was caving in. Although his words reach great heights of personal drama, they are similar to what many could say – many who, like him, have ignored their internal existence.

I believe that one of the great battlegrounds of our age is the private world of the individual. There is a contest that must be fought particularly by those who call themselves practising or observant Christians. Among them are those who work hard, shouldering massive responsibilities at home, at work, and at church. They are good people, but they are very, very tired! And thus they too often live on the verge of a sinkhole-like collapse. Why? Because although their worthwhile actions are very unlike those of Wilde, like him they become too public-world-oriented, ignoring the private side until it is almost too late.

Wayne Muller writes:

> The busier we are, the more important we seem to ourselves and, we imagine, to others. To be unavailable to our friends and family, to be unable to find time for the sunset (or even to know that the sun has set at all), to whiz through our obligations without time for a single mindful breath, this has become the model of a successful life.[2]

Our Western cultural values have helped to blind us to this tendency. We are naively inclined to believe that the most publicly active person is the most privately spiritual. We assume that the larger the church, the greater its heavenly blessing. The more information about the Bible a person possesses, we think, the closer he or she must be to God.

Because we tend to think like this, there is the temptation to give imbalanced attention to our public worlds at the expense of the private. More programs, more meetings, more learning experiences, more relationships, more busyness; until it all becomes so heavy at the surface of life that the whole thing trembles on the verge of collapse. Fatigue, disillusionment, failure, defeat all become frightening possibilities. The neglected private world can no longer hold the weight.

I bump into a man who has claimed Christian faith for a number of years. In the course of our conversation, I ask him one of those questions that Christians ought to ask each other but feel odd in doing so.

I say, "Tell me, how are you doing spiritually?"

He responds, "Interesting question! What's a good answer? Oh, I'm okay, I guess. I wish I could say I was growing or feeling closer to God. But the truth is that I'm sort of standing still."

He gives the impression of wanting to pursue the matter, and so I throw in another question.

"Are you taking time regularly to order your inner life?"

He looks at me inquisitively. If I had used an old Christian term such as, "How's your quiet time?" he would have known exactly how to answer. That would have been measurable, and he could have responded in terms of days, hours, and minutes, systems and techniques. But I had asked about the order of his inner life. And the key word is *order*, a word of *quality*, not quantity. Now he shows discomfort.

"When does a guy ever get to order his inner life? I've got work piled up to keep me going for the rest of the year. I'm out every night this week. My wife is after me to take a week's vacation. The house needs painting. So there's not too much time to think about 'ordering the inner life,' as you put it."

He pauses for a moment and then asks, "What is the inner life anyway?"

Now that's a showstopper of a question. Think of it! Here is a professing Christian who has "done church" for years, has gained a Christian reputation for doing Christian things, but has never pondered the possibility that, underneath all the action and well-meaning religious noise, there has got to be something solid, something dependable. That he sees himself as too busy to maintain an inner world, and that he is not sure he knows what it is anyway tells me that he may have missed by a significant distance the central point of a life in touch with God. You could say that we had a lot to talk about in the following hour.

Few people wrestled with the pressures of a public world more than Anne Morrow Lindbergh, wife of

Charles, the famous aviator. And she jealously guarded her private world and wrote some insightful comments about it in her classic book *The Gift from the Sea:*

> I want first of all . . . to be at peace with myself. I want a singleness of eye, a purity of intention, a central core to my life that will enable me to carry out these obligations and activities as well as I can. I want, in fact – to borrow from the language of the saints – to live "in grace" as much of the time as possible. I am not using this term in a strictly theological sense. By grace I mean an inner harmony, essentially spiritual, which can be translated into outward harmony. I am seeking perhaps what Socrates asked for in the prayer from the Phaedrus when he said, "May the outward and inward man be one." I would like to achieve a state of inner spiritual grace from which I could function and give as I was meant to in the eye of God.[3]

Fred Mitchell, a leader in world missions, used to keep a motto on his desk that read, "Beware of the Barrenness of a Busy Life." He too understood the potential collapse that follows when the inner world is ignored.

The Florida sinkhole is a physical picture of a spiritual problem with which many Western Christians must deal. As the pressure of life continues to grow in the first years of the twenty-first century, there will be more people whose lives resemble a sinkhole, unless they gaze inward and ask themselves, Is there a private world beneath the noise and action at the surface? A world that needs to be explored and maintained? Can strength and resilience be developed that will bear up under the growing pressure at the surface?

In a lonely moment in Washington when John Quincy Adams was overwhelmed by homesickness for his Massachusetts family, he wrote them a letter, addressing comments of encouragement and counsel to each son and daughter. To his daughter he wrote about the prospect of marriage and the kind of man she should choose to marry. His words reveal how highly he regarded an ordered private world:

> Daughter! Get you an honest man for a husband and keep him honest. No matter whether he is rich, provided he be independent. Regard the honour and moral character of the man, more than all other circumstances. *Think of no other greatness but that of the soul, no other riches but those of the heart.* [italics added][4]

MEMO TO THE DISORGANIZED

If my private world is in order, it will be because I make a daily choice to monitor its state of orderliness.

TWO

A View from the Bridge

A FRIEND WAS ONCE AN OFFICER ABOARD A UNITED STATES Navy nuclear submarine. He related to me an experience that happened one day while the sub was on duty in the Mediterranean. Many ships were passing overhead on the surface, and the submarine was forced to make a large number of violent manoeuvres to avoid possible collisions.

In the absence of the captain, my friend was duty officer, in charge of giving the commands by which the submarine was positioned at each moment. Because there was such a sudden and unusual amount of movement, the captain, who had been in his own quarters, suddenly appeared on the bridge asking, "Is everything all right?"

"Yes, sir!" was my friend's reply. The captain took a quick look around and then started back out through the hatch to leave the bridge. As he disappeared he said, "It looks all right to me too." With just a few words and the abrupt exit, the captain conveyed his unqualified confidence in the duty officer's leadership.

That simple, routine encounter between a naval commander and one of his trusted officers provided me with a helpful picture of the order of one's private world. All around that submarine the potential danger of collision was lurking. It was enough to make any alert captain show concern. But that danger was outside. Down deep inside the sub was a quiet place where there could be absolute control of the ship's destiny. And that was where the captain instinctively headed.

On the bridge, the centre of command, there was not a hint of panic; only a calm and deliberate series of actions being carried out by a highly trained crew of seamen doing their jobs. Thus when the commander appeared on the bridge to assure himself that everything was in order, it was. "Is everything all right?" he asked. Assured that it was, he looked about and agreed, "It looks all right to me too." He had gone to the right place and received the proper answer.

That is how the captain organized his sub. The appropriate procedures were practised a thousand times when there was no danger. Thus, when it was time for action in a precarious situation, there was no need for the captain to overreact. He could anticipate an excellent performance from the people on the bridge. When things are in order there, the submarine is secure no matter what the external circumstances. "It looks all right to me too," says the captain.

But there have been cases in which those procedures have been ignored, perhaps left unpractised. Then there can be disaster. Then ships collide and sink, causing great loss.

And so it is with human life when there is disorganization on the "bridge" of the inner world. The accidents that occur there have names like burnout, breakdown, or blowup.

It is one thing for a person to make a mistake, or even to fail. We learn our best lessons of procedure and character under such conditions. But it is another thing to watch human beings disintegrate before our very eyes because there were no resources of interior support in the midst of the pressure.

The *Wall Street Journal* once offered a series of articles entitled "Executive's Crisis," and one story featured Jerald H. Maxwell, a young entrepreneur who founded a hi-tech company and immediately led it to high profitability. For a while he was celebrated as a managerial genius. But, unfortunately, just for a while. A sudden downturn in the economy changed everything. The company's stock cratered, as they say, and the board of directors was forced to take drastic action:

> The day is etched into Jerald H. Maxwell's memory. His family will never forget it, either. To them it is the day he started weeping in his room, the day his exuberant self-confidence ended and his depression began, the day his world – and theirs – came tumbling down.

Maxwell had been fired! Everything in his life seemed to fall apart, and he appeared to lack the inner resources to handle the situation. The *Journal* continued:

> For the first time in his life, Mr. Maxwell was a failure, and it shattered him. His feeling of defeat led to an emotional breakdown, gnawed away at the bonds between Mr. Maxwell and his wife and four sons and pushed him to the brink. "When things fell apart, they felt so bad I was ashamed," Mr. Maxwell recalls. He pauses and sighs, then goes on: "It says in the Bible that all you have to do is ask and you will receive. Well, I asked for death many times."[1]

Most of us have never wished for death as Maxwell did. But more than a few of us have experienced the same pressure from the outer world, crowding in upon us to such an extent that we wondered if some sort of death would not be desirable. During such moments we ask ourselves about the strength of our reserves – whether or not we can keep on going, whether it is worth it to keep pressing, whether it may be time to "cut and run." In short, we are not sure that there is enough spiritual, psychic, or physical energy to keep moving at the pace we are presently trying to maintain.

I've been where Maxwell was in his darkest hours. Our stories are a bit different, but the feelings are not. For a few hours, perhaps for a few days (for some a lot longer than that), there is a numbness. All the resolve is gone. Self-confidence disappears. It seems as if there will be no tomorrow.

It's in the moments that Jerald Maxwell faced, moments that I once knew, that one is forced to the very bottom of one's soul. Is there anything there? The answer to the question will be based on whether or not something has been stored there in better days.

Back to the submarine. Recall, once more, what the captain of that submarine did. When there was a sense of violent turbulence all around, he headed for the bridge to determine whether or not things were in order. The answer, he knew, would be found nowhere else. And if everything was all right there, he knew he could retire to his quarters with confidence. The ship could handle the turbulent circumstances if everything was all right on the bridge.

If you please, another sea story. One of my favourite Bible tales tells of the afternoon Jesus' disciples found themselves in a raging storm on the Sea of Galilee. Soon they were terrified and had lost all of their composure. Here were men who had fished this sea for years, who had their own equipment, and who must have seen such storms before. But for some reason, this time they were not able to handle the situation. Jesus, on the other hand, was asleep in the rear of the boat, and they ran to Him, furious that He seemed not to care that loss of life was a real threat. Perhaps we should at least credit them with knowing where to run.

After Christ had pressed peace into the storm, He asked the question that was central to all of their personal growth and development as spiritual leaders: "Where is your faith?" He could have asked in language I have been using, "Why isn't the bridge of your private world in better order?"

Why is it that for so many the answer to personal tension and pressure lies not in going to the bridge of life but rather in attempting to run faster, protest more vigorously, accumulate more, collect more data, and gain more expertise? We are of an age in which it seems instinctive to give attention to every cubic inch of life other than our inner worlds – the only place from which we can gain the strength to brave, or even beat, any outer turbulence.

Biblical writers believed in the principle of going to the bridge; they knew and taught that the development and maintenance of our inner worlds should be our highest priority. That is one practical reason that their work has transcended all times and cultures. For what they wrote they received from the Creator who made us to work most effectively from the inner world toward the outer. Stephen Covey calls it "the inside-out approach."

One writer of Proverbs put the principle of the inner world in these words: "Watch over your heart with all diligence, for from it flow the springs of life" (Prov. 4:23).

In one simple sentence the writer has conveyed to us a most amazing insight. What I call the "bridge," he calls the "heart." His metaphor for the heart is a spring, and suggests that out of it can flow the energy, the insight, and the force that do not succumb to outer turbulence but rather overcome it. Guard the heart, he says, and it will become a wellspring of life from which you and others can drink.

But what does it mean to "guard" the heart? For one thing, the writer is obviously concerned that the heart be protected from influences outside itself that might jeopardize its integrity. The writer is also focused on the strength and development of the heart in order to increase its capacity to bring order to one's life.

But the writer's thinking goes beyond these two ideas. He wants the reader to understand that keeping or guarding the heart, this thing I've referred to as the "bridge" in the human experience, is a deliberate and disciplined choice a man or woman must make. Am I being heard? We must *choose* to keep the heart. Choose! Its health and productivity cannot be assumed; it must be constantly protected and maintained.

Again, we need to remember what the captain of the submarine did when he felt something out of the ordinary going on: He immediately headed for the bridge. Why? Because he knew that that was the place in which all capability to face danger would be found. He could have commanded the spiffiest submarine in the U.S. Navy in terms of its exterior paint job, its capability for speed, and the congeniality of its crew. But if the bridge was in a state of disorder, all the rest – the paint job, the capacity for speed, and the nice guys on board – would have been meaningless.

In the New Testament, Paul made the same sort of observation when he challenged Christians to "not be conformed to this [outer] world, but be transformed by the renewing of your mind" (Rom. 12:2). He's talking heart here. I've always preferred J. B. Phillip's version of this verse: "Don't let the world squeeze you into its mould."

The great apostle set forth an ageless truth when he wrote this. He was directing his readers to make a right choice. Are we going to order our inner worlds, our hearts, so that they will radiate influence into the outer world? Or will we neglect our private worlds and thus permit the outer influences to shape us? This is a choice we have to make every day of our lives.

This is an incredible thought, and it defines a core Biblical issue. It is the sort of insight that the terminated executive in the *Wall Street Journal* article had ignored. The evidence? His cave-in, when the world about him faced him with crushing pressure. He had no resource of inner strength from which to draw, no order to his private world.

A great name in modern missionary biography is Mary Slessor. Slessor was a young single woman who left Scotland at the turn of the twentieth century to go to a part of Africa that was then infested with disease and indescribable danger. The woman had an indomitable spirit and kept going when lesser men and women, living under the crushing pressures, broke down, ran, and never came back. Once, after a particularly draining day, she found herself trying to sleep in a crude jungle hut. Of that night she wrote:

> I am not very particular about my bed these days, but as I lay on a few dirty sticks laid across and covered with a litter of dirty corn-shells, with plenty of rats and insects, three women and an infant three days old alongside, and over a dozen sheep and goats and cows outside, you don't wonder that I slept little. *But I had such a comfortable quiet night in my own heart.* [italics added][2]

Now that is the sort of thing we are thinking about when we address the question of order in our private worlds. Whether you call it the "bridge" in naval language or the "heart" in biblical language, the point is the same: There must be a quiet place where all is in order, a place from which comes the energy that overcomes turbulence and is not intimidated by it.

Although he wasn't trying to make a uniquely Christian point, I nevertheless find the words of Ralph Waldo Emerson quite provocative. "It is easy in the world," he wrote, "to live after the world's opinion; it is easy in solitude to live after our own; but the great man is he who in the midst of the crowd keeps with perfect sweetness the independence of solitude."

Emerson is talking heart language here.

We will know that we have learned this significant principle when we come to the point at which the development and maintenance of a strong inner world becomes the most important single function of our existences. Then in the moment when pressure rises and tension increases, we can look within and ask, "Is everything all right?" And discovering that it is, we can say, "It looks all right to me too."

Sector One

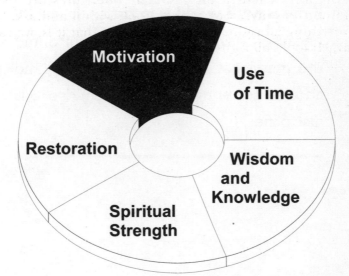

Motivation

Use of Time

Restoration

Wisdom and Knowledge

Spiritual Strength

MEMO TO THE DISORGANIZED

If my private world is in order, it will be because I have courageously confronted the messiness of my ways of living and chosen to bring them under rigorous discipline.

THREE

Caught in a Golden Cage

THE TWELVE MEN WHO FOLLOWED JESUS CHRIST AND later launched the church that bears His name were a curious and unpredictable group. There is not one of them (with the possible exception of Judas Iscariot, who, it has to be admitted, appeared to have a mind for practicality) I would have picked to lead a movement like the one Jesus clearly had in mind. No, I would not have picked any of them. But Jesus did, and His choices, Judas excluded, are unimpeachable.

Now there were, in fact, others who showed signs of enthusiasm in their desire to join Jesus' movement. Being a bit assertive myself – a proactive type, as they say – I am fascinated by these volunteers and would have been inclined to include them. But Jesus wasn't, and He discouraged them. I wish I knew why. His responses to their initiatives seem harsh at first light (Luke 9:57ff) and suggest that Jesus rebuffed them because He had reservations about them that the gospel writers do not fully reveal.

Is it possible that Jesus, with His extraordinary intuition, looked into their private worlds and saw danger signs? Let me make an attempt at reading Jesus' mind and propose that He sensed what one might call drivenness, a quality seen in people motivated to make something of themselves for less-than-best reasons.

Maybe the clue is in the fact that you see them wanting to place conditions on their discipleship by stipulating *when* they would engage with Jesus and *what* they might want out of the relationship. Just speculations, to be sure, but worth thinking about.

Perhaps (I'm brainstorming here) if they had come aboard we would have discovered that they had a lot more in their personal agendas than was apparent at first. We would have found that they were men with their own plans and schemes, goals, and objectives. And Jesus Christ would not do mighty works in the private worlds of people who were so driven. He never did then, and He won't now.

In contrast to those who are driven are the *called*. There's a bit of vagueness in this, but it would appear that there were certain people who began to hang out with Jesus. They listened intently when He spoke; watched carefully when He acted; responded seriously when He asked questions. And then, perhaps when it was least expected, He called or invited them into His tight microcommunity of followers. To this group He gave enormous amounts of time and attention. And they were transformed.

In an exploration of the inner sphere of the person, one has to begin somewhere, so I have chosen to begin where Christ appears to have begun – this distinction between the *called* and the *driven*.

Let's take a hard look at drivenness. It's worth some thought because too many of us find ourselves falling into this category. And we're not real happy about it.

How can you spot a driven person? Today it is relatively easy. Start with the signs of stress, and you have probably found some driven men and women. Not always, of course. But it's worth beginning here.

In recent years it has become very clear that many people in our society are under constant and destructive stress as life for them operates at a pace that offers little time for any restorative rest and retreat. The costs related to stress are astronomical in the health-care industry as we discover its links to heart disease, cancer, lung ailments, accidental injuries, cirrhosis of the liver, and suicide.

I belong to the generation that saw stress become the serious malady it is today. People worked hard in the days of my childhood, very hard. But they generally knew when to stop working, when to sit on the porch and listen to the ball game, when to take a walk and visit friends, when to get a decent night's sleep. Sure, people got tired. But they didn't constantly complain of the exhaustion we hear about today.

Has it occurred to you how often we talk about our fatigue? I sometimes have the feeling that if I don't tell my friends how tired I am they will doubt I am doing anything worthwhile. Try telling someone that you feel great, that you are at the top of your game, that you've never been better. The chances are that they will suspect that you're putting them on . . . that you lack sincerity.

How did we get to a day when stress and fatigue are almost a badge of success?

We are all aware that there is a kind of stress that is beneficial because it brings out the best in performers, athletes, or executives. But most of the attention presently being given to the subject centres on the kinds of stress that diminish rather than enhance human capacity.

One fascinating study on stress was conducted by the late Dr. Thomas Holmes. Holmes was known for his development of the famous Social Readjustment Rating Scale, or as most of us know it, the Holmes Stress Chart. Holmes's stress chart is a simple measurement device that indicates how much pressure a person is probably facing and how close he may be to dangerous physical and psychic consequences.

After considerable research, various events common to all of us were assigned point totals by Holmes and his associates. Each point was called a "life-change unit." An accumulation of more than 200 of these units in any one year, Holmes suggested, could be the warning of a potential heart attack, emotional stress, or breakdown of the ability to function as a healthy person. The death of a spouse, for example, commands the highest number of life-change units, 100. Being fired from a job produces 47 points, while the acquisition of a new family member provides 39. Not all stress-producing events listed by Holmes are negative. Even positive and happy events such as Christmas (12 points) and vacations (13) create stress.

My experience is that it is not unusual to talk with people whose point totals well beyond 200. A pastor, for example, comes to visit with me at my office. His point total, he tells me, is 324. His blood pressure is dangerously high; he suffers from constant stomach pains, he fears an ulcer, and he does not sleep well at night. On another day, I sit at breakfast with a young executive who admits that until recently his ambition had been to accumulate a minimum of a million dollars before the age of thirty. When he matches his present situation up against the Holmes Stress Chart, he is horrified to discover that his point total is 412. What do these two men from the business and religious world have in common?

These are what I call *driven* men. And their drive is costing them terribly – the point totals are simply a numerical indication of that fact. I use the word driven because it describes not only the condition in which they are pursuing life, but also because it is descriptive of the way many of the rest of us are not facing up to the reality of what we are doing to ourselves. Perhaps we are being driven toward goals and objectives without always understanding why. Or we may not be aware of the real cost to our minds, our bodies, and, of course, our hearts. By heart I mean the one written about in Proverbs 4:23, that fountainhead from which comes the energy of life.

There are lots of driven people doing very good things. Driven people are not necessarily bad folk, although the consequences of their drivenness may produce unfortunate results. In fact, driven people often make great contributions. They start organizations; they provide jobs and opportunities; they are often very bright and offer ways and means of doing things that benefit many other people. Nevertheless they are driven, and one worries about their ability to sustain the pace without danger to themselves.

In another book of mine, I related a story from the writings of Mrs. Charles Cowman, whose spiritual reflections were quite popular fifty or more years ago. A nineteenth-century explorer, she wrote, had hired a group of African villagers to provide support for his exploration of a portion of unmapped Africa. On the first three days of their trek, they achieved an unexpected rate of speed, which put them substantially ahead of schedule. The scientist was elated.

But all that changed on the fourth day when he arose from his tent and discovered that no one was moving. In fact he was told that the African support team intended to sit the day out. When he asked why, he was told that they had decided they'd been moving much too fast and that it was time to stop and let their souls catch up with their bodies.

There's a message in the ageing story. It suggests – in a fascinating way – that it is possible for the public and the private world of a person to split. And the greater the split, the higher the stress. The Africans were wise to this; the explorer hadn't a clue.

Can driven people be spotted? Yes, of course. There are many symptoms that suggest a person is driven. Among the ones I see most often are these:

1. *A driven person is most often gratified only by accomplishment.* Somewhere in the process of maturation this person discovers that the only way he can feel good about himself and his world is to accumulate accomplishments. This discovery may be the result of formative influences at an early age; as a child, affirmation and approval may have been received from a parent or influential mentor only when something had been finished. Nothing of value may have ever been said until that task was completed. Thus the only way he could find love and acceptance was through accomplishment.

I was standing at the entrance of the arena where my granddaughter plays indoor soccer. A small boy, no older than nine, came out the door and spied his father. "I scored a goal, Dad," he said with excitement. "Yeah," his father replied, "but you missed the chance for two others."

This exchange, which happened just a day or two ago, caused me to wonder if I wasn't watching a boy who was being shaped by his father to define life and human value only in terms of accomplishment. You got one, but you could have done *more.* In such ways a lasting message is implanted in the boy's soul, and it is done by an important authority figure.

A psychology of achievement sometimes captures the heart in circumstances like that. A person begins to reason that if one accomplishment resulted in good feelings and the praise of others, then several more accomplishments may bring an abundance of good feelings and affirmations. Or if one accomplishment (in this case a goal) is not good enough, then perhaps three more will gain what I need most: approval.

So the driven person begins to look for ways to accumulate more and more achievements. He will soon be found doing two or three things at one time, because that brings even more of this strange sort of pleasure. He becomes the sort of person who is always reading books and attending seminars that promise to help him use what time he has even more effectively. Why? So that he can produce more accomplishments, which in turn will provide greater gratification.

This is the kind of person who sees life only in terms of results. As such, he has little appreciation for the process leading toward results. This kind of person would love to fly from New York to Los Angeles at supersonic speed, because to travel at ground speed and see the hills of Pennsylvania, the golden wheat of Iowa and Nebraska, the awesomeness of the Rockies, and the deserts of Utah and Nevada would be a terrible waste of time. Upon arrival in Los Angeles after a swift two-hour trip, this driven person would be highly irritated if the plane took four extra minutes to get into the gate. Arrival is everything to this accomplishment-oriented individual; the trip means nothing.

2. *A driven person is preoccupied with the symbols of accomplishment.* He is usually conscious of the concept of power, and he seeks to possess it in order to wield it. That means that he will be aware of the symbols of status: titles, office size and location, positions on organizational charts, and special privileges.

There is generally a concern for one's own notoriety when in a state of drivenness. Who, the driven person wonders, knows about what I am doing? How can I be better connected with the "greats" of my world? These questions often preoccupy the driven person.

3. *A driven person is usually caught in the uncontrolled pursuit of expansion.* Driven people like to be a part of something that is getting bigger and more successful.

They are usually on the move, seeking the biggest and the best opportunities. They rarely have any time to appreciate the achievements to date.

The nineteenth-century English preacher Charles Spurgeon once said:

> Success exposes a man to the pressures of people and thus tempts him to hold on to his gains by means of fleshly methods and practices, and to let himself be ruled wholly by the dictatorial demands of incessant expansion. Success can go to my head and will unless I remember that it is God who accomplishes the work, that he can continue to do so without my help, and that he will be able to make out with other means whenever he wants to cut me out.[1]

You can see this unfortunate principle in the pursuit of some careers. But you can also see it in the context of spiritual activity, for there is such a thing as a spiritually driven person who is never satisfied with who he is or what he accomplishes in religious work. And of course this means that his attitude toward those around him is much the same. He is rarely pleased with the progress of his peers or subordinates. He lives in a constant state of uneasiness and restlessness, looking for more efficient methods, greater results, deeper spiritual experiences. There is usually no sign that he will ever be satisfied with himself or anyone else.

Here in North America we now live in what I call the era of the visionary church. Almost every pastor is judged on the basis of whether he/she has a vision. And this usually means a vision of how the church can grow, grow, grow. The pastoral care of the people – which for hundreds of years has been the aim of a church – is less important in comparison to the gathering of more people. Because more people means more programs, more buildings, more employed staff. Doubtless this is not all bad if it results in bringing unchurched people into the kingdom of God. But one wants to watch a lot of this "vision" and ask how much of it is satisfying the need of a driven leader who has to see things expand at all costs.

My speculation will probably irritate some. But even if I appear to have exaggerated my point, it will not hurt to take a second look at what we assume to be blessing if we discover it was fuelled by drivenness and not by calledness.

4. Driven people tend to have a limited regard for integrity.
They can become so preoccupied with success and achievement that they have little time to stop and ask if their inner person is keeping pace with the outer process. Usually it is not, and there is an increasing gap, a breakdown in integrity. People like this often become progressively deceitful; and they not only deceive others, but they also deceive themselves. In the attempt to push ahead relentlessly, they lie to themselves about motives; values and morals are compromised. Shortcuts to success become a way of life. Because the goal is so important, they drift into ethical shabbiness. Driven people become frighteningly pragmatic.

5. Driven people are not likely to bother themselves with the honing of people skills. They are not noted for creating environments in which it is a pleasure for others to work. The truth is that programs, projects, and tasks are more important to them than people. Because their eyes are upon goals and objectives, they are rarely sensitive to the people about them, except as they can be used for the fulfilment of one of the goals. And if others are not found to be useful, then they may be seen as obstacles or competitors when it comes to getting something done.

There is usually a "trail of bodies" in the wake of the driven person. Where once others praised him for his seemingly great leadership, there soon appears a steady increase in frustration and hostility, as they see that the driven person cares very little about the health and growth of human beings. It becomes apparent that there is a non-negotiable agenda, and it is supreme above all other things. Colleagues and subordinates in the orbit of the driven person slowly drop away, one after another, exhausted, exploited, and disillusioned. Of this person we are most likely to find ourselves saying, "He is miserable to work with, but he certainly gets things done."

And therein lies the rub. He gets things done, but he may destroy people in the process. Not an attractive sight. Yet the ironic thing, which cannot be ignored, is that in almost every great organization, religious and secular, people of this sort can be found in key positions. Even though they carry with them the seeds of relational disaster, they often are indispensable to the action.

One day, many years ago, I was in the lobby of our church having a conversation with one of our staff members. A woman, Marilyn, came through the front entrance. Marilyn struggled with mental difficulties and was always highly medicated. In her somewhat dazed state she often seemed a drain on people because she talked slowly and raised topics unimportant to busy people . . . like me (I am ashamed to say).

Seeing Marilyn, I called across the lobby, "Hello, Marilyn. How are you?" and then quickly turned back to my conversation with the staff member in the hope that she would realize I was busy and not intrude.

But that was not to be. Suddenly I was aware that Marilyn was approaching, in fact inserting herself between me and my conversation partner. Looking up at me – she was a very short woman – she said in her slow, medicated, and flat tone of voice, "Pastor Mac, you say, 'Hello, Marilyn. How are you?' but you really do not want to know. You are too busy to pay attention to someone like me. I'm just not important enough."

And Marilyn was right! Perhaps a score of other people felt the same way but didn't have the courage to say it in the same way. Marilyn's medications suspended those social "graces" that keep us from saying what we are thinking and caused her to say the exact truth. I could only apologize to her and ponder the evidence that I suffered from drivenness to a considerable extent.

6. *Driven people tend to be highly competitive. They see each effort as a win-or-lose situation.* And, of course, the driven person feels he must win, must look good before others. The more driven he is, the larger the score by which he needs to win. Winning provides the evidence the driven person desperately needs that he is right, valuable, and important. Thus, he is likely to see others as competitors or as enemies who must be beaten – perhaps even humiliated – in the process.

A man comes to mind with whom I played board games from time to time when I was a boy. It was not only important to him that he win but that he win big, as they say. If we played Monopoly, he would bankrupt me and then (stretching the rules) loan me money to keep on playing so that I could lose a second time. If we were playing Scrabble, he would run up the score with his far superior vocabulary and keep me struggling in the game even though I had lost heart and interest a long time ago. To this day, board games are something I will do anything to avoid (much to my wife's chagrin). The echoes of the repeated humiliations years ago remain with me. Driven people do this to others. And shouldn't!

7. *A driven person often possesses a volcanic force of anger,* which can erupt anytime he senses opposition or disloyalty. This anger can be triggered when people

disagree, offer an alternative solution to a problem, or even hint at just a bit of criticism.

The anger may not surface as physical violence. But it can take the form of verbal brutality: profanity or humiliating insults, for example. The anger can express itself in vindictive acts such as firing people, slandering them before peers, or simply denying them things they have come to expect, such as affection, money, or even companionship.

Frankly, I would not have believed the story had it not been told by a person I trust. Picture an open office of a small business with several working associates. The office manager, a woman who has worked in the office for fifteen years, has made a request to the business-owner for a week off to be with a sick baby. When he refuses, she responds tearfully, asking him to reconsider. Big mistake! When he sees her tears, he snarls, "Clean out your desk and get out of here; I don't need you anyhow." When she is gone he turns to the horrified onlookers and says, "Let's get one thing straight; you're all here for only one reason: to make money for this business. And if you don't like that, get out right now!"

Tragically, many good people who surround the driven person are more than willing to absorb the impact of such anger although it desperately hurts them, because they reason that the boss or the leader is good at what he or she does. Sometimes the anger and its cruel effects are accepted simply because no one has either the courage or the ability to stand up to the driven person.

Recently a person who serves on the board of a major Christian organization told me of encounters with the executive director that included outbursts of rage studded with extraordinary profanity and demeaning language. When I asked why board members accepted this form of behaviour, which was neither rare nor open to excuse, he said, "I guess we were so impressed with the way God seemed to use him in his public ministry that we were reluctant to confront him."

Is there anything else worth saying about the driven person, who by now appears to be entirely unlikeable? Yes, simply this:

8. *Driven people are usually abnormally busy, are averse to play, and usually avoid spiritual worship.* They are usually too busy for the pursuit of ordinary relationships in marriage, family, or friendship, or even to carry on a relationship with themselves – not to speak of one with God. Because driven people rarely think they have accomplished enough, they seize every available minute to attend more meetings, to study more material, to initiate more projects. They operate on the precept that a reputation for busyness is a sign of success and personal importance. Thus they attempt to impress people with the fullness of their schedules. They may even express a high level of self-pity, bemoaning the "trap" of responsibility they claim to be in, wishing aloud that there was some possible release from all that they have to live with. But just try to suggest a way out!

The truth is that the very worst thing that could happen to them would be if someone provided them with a way out. They really wouldn't know what to do with themselves if there were suddenly less to do. Busyness for the driven person becomes a habit, a way of life and thought. They find it enjoyable to complain and gather pity, and they would probably not want it any different. But tell a driven person that, and you'll make him angry.

This then is the driven person – not an entirely attractive picture. What often disturbs me as I look at this picture is the fact that much of our world is run by driven people. We have created a system that rides on their backs. And where that is true in businesses, in churches, and in homes, the growth of people is often sacrificed for accomplishment and accumulation.

Pastors who are driven men or women have been known to burn out scores of assistants and lay leaders because of their need to head organizations that are the biggest, the best, and the most well known. There are businesspeople who claim Christian faith and who have enjoyed a reputation for graciousness in the church, but who are ruthless in the office, pushing people and squeezing them for the last ounce of energy simply so they themselves can enjoy the gratification of winning, accumulating, or establishing a reputation.

Among the more painful self-revelations of my life was that I am basically a driven person. I have, at one time or another, seen in myself almost all of the traits I have listed. That drivenness has created moments of crisis for me down through the years. And each time I had to come to grips with fresh new revelations of an insidious energy within me that wanted to achieve and accomplish things for reasons that were far from obedience to Jesus or the glory of God.

What I had to learn was that my drivenness needed to be consecrated on a daily basis. I had to listen to my wife and to those closest to me to see if they saw any of the signs of uncontrolled drivenness. I had to engage in regular self-examination to assure that the plans I was making, the leadership I was giving, the goals I was setting were more in alignment with calledness than drivenness. I had to learn how to listen to God and assure that I was moving according to His agenda and not my self-serving one. To ignore the possibility that my life could be taken over by the spirit of drivenness would be to my peril.

Some time ago a businessman became a Christian through the witness of a layman who is a good friend of mine. Not long after making his choice to follow Jesus Christ, he wrote a long letter to my friend who had guided him into faith. In it he described some of his struggles as the result of his driven condition. I requested permission to share part of the letter because it so vividly illustrated the driven person. He wrote:

> Several years ago I was at a point of great frustration in my life. Although I had a wonderful wife and three beautiful sons, my career was going badly. I had few friends, my oldest son began getting into trouble – he started failing in school – I was suffering from depression, there was great tension and unhappiness in my family. At that time I had an opportunity to travel overseas where I stayed to work in a foreign company. This new opportunity was such an excellent one, financially and career-wise, that I made it number one in my life, forsaking all other values. I did many wrong (i.e., sinful) things to advance my position and success. I justified them as being of good consequence to my family (more money, etc.), which resulted in my lying to myself and my family and behaving wrongly in many ways.

> Of course this was intolerable to my wife, and she and my family returned to the U.S. I was still blind, however, to the problems that were within me. My success, my salary, my career, all moved upward. *I was caught in a golden cage.* [italics mine]

> Although many wonderful things were happening outside me, inside I was losing everything. My capacity to reason and my capacity to decide were both weakened. I would evaluate alternatives, constantly going over various options, always trying to pick the one that would maximize success and career. I knew in my heart that something was terribly wrong. I went to church, but the words there couldn't reach me. I was too caught up in my own world.

> After a terrible episode with my family several weeks ago, I completely gave up my course of thinking and went to a hotel room for nine days to figure out what to do. The more I thought, the more troubled I became. I began to realize how dead I really was, how so much of my life was dark. And worse than that, I could see no way out. My only solution was to run and hide, to start in a different place, to sever all connections.

This brutal description of a man at the bottom fortunately has a happy ending. For not long after his nine-day experience in a hotel room, he discovered the love of God and its capacity to engender dramatic change in his life. And a driven man turned into what we will call in our next chapter a *called man*. He got out of his "golden cage."

In the Bible few men typify the driven man better than Saul, the first king of Israel. Unlike the previous story, which had a happy conclusion, this one has a miserable ending, for Saul never got out of his golden cage. All he did was heap increasing amounts of stress upon himself. And it destroyed him.

The Bible's introduction to Saul should be warning enough that the man had some flaws that, if not addressed within his inner world, would cause him quickly to lose personal control.

> There was a man of Benjamin whose name was Kish the son of Abiel, the son of Zeror, the son of Becorath, the son of Aphiah, the son of a Benjamite, a mighty man of valor. And he had a son whose name was Saul, a choice and handsome man, and there was not a more handsome person than he among the sons of Israel; from his shoulders and up he was taller than any of the people. (1 Sam. 9:1-2)

Saul possessed three unearned characteristics at the beginning of his public life that had the potential to become assets or serious liabilities. Which they would be was his choice. And how Saul made those choices depended upon the daily order of his private world.

The three characteristics? First, wealth; second, an attractive appearance; and third, a physically large and well-developed body. All were attributes of a person's public world. In other words, the initial impression was that Saul was a better man than anyone around him. All three external marks commanded attention and gained him quick advantages. (Each time I think of Saul's natural gifts, I recall the bank president some years ago who said to me, "MacDonald, you could go a long way in the business world if you were about six inches taller.") And, most importantly, they provided him with a sort of charisma that made possible his achieving some early success without ever having to develop a heart of wisdom or spiritual stature. He was simply a fast starter.

As Saul's story unfolds in the biblical text, we learn some other things about the man, things that could have either contributed to his success or become a part of his ultimate failure. We are told, for example, that he was good with words. When he was given a chance to speak before crowds, he was eloquent. The stage was set for a man to consolidate power and command recognition without ever having to develop any sense of a strong inner world first. And that was where the danger lay.

When Saul became king of Israel, he enjoyed too much immediate success. It apparently made him unaware that he had any limits to his life. He spent little time pondering his need for others, engendering a relationship with God, or even facing his responsibilities toward the people over whom he ruled. The signs of a driven man began to appear.

Saul became a busy man; he saw worlds he thought needed conquering. Thus, when he faced an impending battle with the Philistines, Israel's great enemy of the day, and waited at Gilgal for Samuel the prophet to come and offer the necessary sacrifices, he grew impatient and irritable when the holy man did not arrive on time. Saul felt that his timetable was being compromised; he had to get on with things. His remedy? Offer the sacrifice himself. And that is exactly what he did.

The result? A rather serious breach of covenant with God. Offering sacrifice was the kind of thing prophets like Samuel did, not kings like Saul. But Saul had forgotten that because he saw himself as being too important.

From that time forward Saul found himself on a downhill track. "Now your kingdom shall not endure. The Lord has sought out for Himself a man after His own heart" (1 Sam. 13:14). This is how most driven men end.

Stripped of what blessing and assistance he had had from God up to this point, Saul's drivenness began to reveal itself even further. Soon all of his energies became consumed in holding on to his throne, competing with young David, who had caught the imagination of the people of Israel.

The Scriptures give several examples of Saul's explosive anger, which drove him to outrage as well as to moments of paralyzing self-pity. By the end of his life, he was a man out of control, seeing enemies behind every bush. Why? Because from the very beginning Saul had been a driven man, and he had never cultivated the order of his private world.

I wonder what Saul's point total would have been on Thomas Holmes's stress chart. I suspect it would have been up in the range of stroke and heart attack victims. But Saul never came to grips with his drivenness, either through something like a stress chart or by simply facing the inner rebukes God would have liked for him to have heard within his private world. Saul would not have lasted long among the twelve disciples Jesus picked. His own compulsions were far too strong. That which had driven him to grasp power and not let go, that which had caused him to turn on his closest supporters, and that which caused him to make a successive series of unwise decisions, finally led him to a humiliating death. He was the classic driven man.

To the extent that we see him in ourselves, we have work to do in our private worlds. For an inner life fraught with unresolved drives will not be able to hear clearly the voice of Christ when He calls. The noise and pain of stress will be too great.

Unfortunately, our society abounds with Sauls, men and women caught in golden cages, driven to accumulate, to be recognized, or to achieve. Our churches, unfortunately, abound with these driven people as well. Many churches are fountains gone dry. Rather than being springs of life-giving energy that cause people to grow and to delight in God's way, they become sources of stress. The driven man's private world is disordered. His cage may be lavishly golden. But it's a trap; inside there is nothing that lasts.

MEMO TO THE DISORGANIZED

If my private world is in order, it will be because, having faced up to what drives me, I listen quietly for the call of Christ.

FOUR

The Tragic Tale of a Successful Bum

WHEN THE COUPLE CAME INTO MY OFFICE FOR THE FIRST of a series of visits, they chose seats on the couch that placed them as far apart from one another as possible. It was obvious that neither liked the other, at least at the moment. And yet the agenda was the saving of their marriage.

She was asking him to leave the home, I was told. When I asked her why, she said it was the only possible way there would be any peace or normal life for the rest of the family. There was no infidelity, no single issue. She simply wasn't prepared to live with him for the rest of his life, given his temperament and value system.

But he didn't want to leave. In fact he was shocked that she should have come to this conclusion, he said. After all, he was a faithful provider; their home was quite large and located in an affluent neighbourhood. The kids had everything they wanted. It was hard to figure out, he went on, why she would want to end the marriage. Besides, weren't they Christians? He'd thought all along that Christians didn't believe in divorce or separation. Would I please solve their problem?

The story slowly emerged. It became clear that I was visiting with one of those driven men and his wife. His drivenness was costing him a marriage, a family, and, additionally, his physical health. That the marriage was virtually dead I could see in their body language. That the family was in ruins I could deduce from their descriptions of the attitudes of the children. That his health was precarious was obvious when he told me of a bundle of ulcers, migraine headaches, and occasional chest pains. The story continued to unfold.

Because he owned his business, he had the freedom to work his own hours: twelve to fifteen per day was all. And because he bore a lot of responsibility, he was rarely at any function important to his children. He usually left the home before anyone was out of bed in the morning, and he rarely came home until the youngest of the children was already back in bed for the night. If he was present at a family meal, he tended to be sullen and preoccupied. It was not a rare occurrence for him to be called to the phone in the middle of dinner and remain there for the remainder of the hour solving some problem or closing a sale.

In moments of conflict, he admitted, he was given to explosive anger; in relationships he could be abrasive and intimidating. Put into a social situation he was usually bored with casual conversation and tended to withdraw and drink too much. When asked who his friends were, he could name no one except business associates. And when challenged as to things of importance apart from his work, he could think only of his sports car, his boat, and his skybox season tickets to the Red Soxthings, not people all of which, ironically, he was usually too busy to enjoy anyway.

This was a man with almost no order at all in his private world. Everything was external. His life was, by his own admission, a bundle of activity and accumulation. He could never do enough; he could never earn enough to be satisfied. Everything had to get bigger, better, and more impressive. What was driving him? Could there ever be order to his private world?

After a number of conversations, I began to gain some insight into the seemingly bottomless energy source that drove this man into a way of life that was destroying everything around him. In the midst of one of our talks, I asked him about his father. Suddenly his mood dramatically altered. Clearly my question had exposed a deeply sensitive matter.

What slowly unfolded was a tale of extreme relational pain. His father, I learned, was a man given to extreme sarcasm and ridicule. He had regularly told his son, "You're a bum; you will always be a bum, nothing better!" He had heard this so many times that the words had become emblazoned as if on a neon sign in the centre of his private world.

Here was a man, now in his mid-forties, who had unconsciously made a lifelong commitment. He had committed himself to proving his father wrong. Somehow he would demonstrate with unimpeachable evidence that he was not a bum. It became a core preoccupation of his life, and he was not even aware of it.

Since a state of "un-bumness" was equated, in his mind, with hard work, high income, and the status of wealth, these things formed the cluster of objectives for this driven man. He would show that he was a hard worker by owning a business and making it the best in that section of the Yellow Pages. He would make sure that it produced large sums of money for him, even if some of the money was "dirtied" by the way it was obtained. The large house, the sports car, the season tickets among the finest boxes at Fenway would all be measurable disclaimers of the paternal charge of "bumness." And thus it was that my visitor became a driven man, driven to earn his father's respect and love.

Because his goals were all basically external, there was no need to cultivate an inner world. Relationships were not important; winning was. Spiritual health was not significant; physical strength was. Rest was not necessary; available time for more work was. And the accumulation of knowledge and wisdom was not a matter of value; sales technique and product innovation were.

He claimed that it was all part of his desire to provide for his family. Slowly we began to discover together that he was really trying to gain his father's affirmation and acceptance. He wanted to hear his father finally say, "Son, you're not a bum; I was really, really wrong."

What made this matter all the more bizarre was that the unpleasable father had been dead for several years. Yet the son, now in midlife, continued to work to gain an imagined approval. What had started as an objective became a habit of living, an addiction you could say, which he could not break.

WHY ARE PEOPLE DRIVEN?

Why do so many people appear to be driven? My friend is an extreme example of one reason. He typifies those who grew up in environments where "well done" was never heard. When such acceptance and affirmation is lacking, it is by no means unusual for the respect-starved person to conclude that more work, greater accumulation of symbols of success, or worldly praise will finally convince some significant person (a parent, for example) who has withheld approval to finally say, "Son (Daughter), you are not a bum after all. I'm terribly proud to be your father."

Many people in leadership positions share this sort of background and this sort of insecurity. Some leaders appear to be highly benevolent people, doing good things, and are praised for dedicated, selfless actions; the fact may be that they are pushed toward the hope of gaining the acceptance and approval of just one significant person in their past. And if they cannot gain that, then they develop an insatiable appetite for applause, wealth, or power from other sources in an attempt to compensate for the loss. Rarely, however, is satisfaction reached. This is because their pursuit is in the public world; the private world is left empty and wanting. And that is where the real ache lies.

Another source of drivenness is an early experience of serious deprivation or shame. In his book *Creative Suffering*[1], Paul Tournier points out that an enormous number of world political leaders over the past several centuries have been orphans. Having grown up in a context of personal loss in terms of intimate parental love and emotional closeness, they may have sought a compensatory experience in the embrace of the crowds. Behind their great drive for power may be the simple need for love. Rather than meeting this need through the ordering of the private world within, they have chosen to pursue it on the external level.

In a revelatory essay Susan Erikson Bloland, daughter of the great twentieth-century psychologist, Erik Erikson, wrote of the drivenness of her father to become a famous and influential man. Erikson, his daughter wrote, never knew who his father was. His mother had refused to disclose his identity. Throughout his lifetime, Erik Erikson drove himself from one achievement to another, imagining that if he did well enough, his father would appear and express admiration to his son.

Driven people can also come from backgrounds in which there has been a sense of great shame or embarrassment. My library includes a remarkably candid book, *The Man Who Could Do No Wrong,* by now-retired pastor Charles Blair. In it he describes his own childhood during the Depression days in Oklahoma. With pain he recalls his daily task of hauling the free government-issue milk from the local firehouse to home. As he carried the milk pail down the street, he had to endure what he felt was raw scorn from boys his own age. Out of the agony of such moments came the resolve that the day would come when he would never again carry a symbolic milk pail, which signified a feeling of worthlessness.

Blair tells the story of an unforgettable walk home from school in the company of a girl for whom he had strong feelings. Suddenly a boy with a shiny new bicycle came up beside them and offered the girl a ride. Without hesitation she hopped on to the back fender, leaving Blair behind as she and the other boy rode off together. The humiliation of that moment caused Blair to quietly resolve that someday *he* would have the equivalent of a shiny bicycle, that *he* would have the wherewithal to make impressions that would command the attentions and loyalties of others.

And those resolves burned their way into his life. They became a source of the drive that subsequently, by his own account, betrayed him. He would later need to own the most attractive automobile, lead the most beautiful and largest church, and wear the most stylish of men's fashions. These things would prove that he had made it out of the Oklahoma Depression. He was not worthless; he was not poor. He could prove it. Look!

Charles Blair was running from something, and that meant that he had to run toward something. Although his drive was clothed in all sorts of impressive spiritual motives, and although his ministry was remarkably effective, down at the centre were unresolved hurts of the past. Because these hurts remained a point of disorder in his private world, they came back to haunt him. They affected his choices and values and blinded him to what was really happening at a crucial moment of his life. The result? Serious disaster. Failure, embarrassment, and public humiliation.

But it must be added that he rebounded. That alone suggests hope for the driven man. Charles Blair, the *driven* man of earlier years, running from shame, is now a called man, and he deserves the admiration of his friends. I consider his book to be one of the most significant I have ever read. It ought to be required reading for any man or woman who is in leadership.

Finally, some people are simply raised in an environment where drivenness is a way of life. In a book called *Wealth Addiction*, Philip Slater details the backgrounds of several living billionaires. In almost every account there is indication that as children these billionaires made the accumulation of things and the conquest of people their amusement. There was little if any play for the purpose of pure fun or exercise. They only knew how to win, how to accumulate. It was what they saw their parents doing, and they assumed that it was the only way to live. Thus the drive to grow rich and powerful began in the earliest days.

To such people an ordered private world has little meaning. The only thing worth giving attention to is the public world, where things can be measured, admired, and used.

Of course, driven people come out of many other backgrounds, and these are but a few samples. But one thing is sure in all cases: Driven people will never enjoy the tranquillity of an ordered private world. Their prime targets are all external, material, and measurable. Nothing else seems real; nothing else makes much sense. And it all must be held on to, as it was with Saul, who found that power was more important than the integrity of a friendship with David.

Let us be sure we understand that when we speak of driven people, we are not merely thinking of a highly competitive businessperson or a professional athlete. We are considering something much more pervasive than workaholism. Any of us can look within and suddenly discover that drivenness is our way of life. We can be driven toward a superior Christian reputation, toward a desire for some dramatic spiritual experience, or toward a form of leadership that is really more a quest for domination of people than servanthood. A homemaker can be a driven person; so can a student. A driven person can be any of us.

HOPE FOR THE DRIVEN PERSON

Can the driven person be changed? Most certainly. It begins when such a person faces up to the fact that he is operating according to drives and not calls. That discovery is usually made in the blinding, searching light of an encounter with Christ. As the twelve disciples discovered, an audience with Jesus over a period of time exposes all the roots and expressions of drivenness.

To deal with drivenness, one must begin to ruthlessly appraise one's own motives and values, just as Peter was forced to do in his periodic confrontations with Jesus. The person seeking relief from drivenness will find it wise to listen to mentors and critics who speak Christ's words to us today.

He may have some humbling acts of renunciation, some disciplined gestures of surrender of thingsthings that are not necessarily bad, but that have been important for all the wrong reasons.

Perhaps the driven person will have to grant forgiveness to some of those who in the past never offered the proper kind of affection and affirmation. And all of that may be just the beginning.

Paul the apostle in his pre-Christian days was driven. As a driven man, he studied, he joined, he attained, he defended, and he was applauded. The pace at which he was operating shortly before his conversion was almost manic. He was driven toward some illusive goal, and later, when he could look back at that lifestyle with all of its compulsions, he would say, "It was all worthless."

Paul was driven until Christ called him. One gets the feeling that when Paul fell to his knees before the Lord while on the road to Damascus, there was an explosion of relief within his private world. What a change from the drivenness that had pushed him toward Damascus in an attempt to stamp out Christianity to that dramatic moment when, in complete submission, he asked Jesus Christ, "What shall I do, Lord?" A driven man was converted into a called one.

I could have wished this for the man who came to talk with me about his wife's demand that he leave their house. Time after time we talked about his insatiable drive to win, to earn, to impress. There were a few occasions when I thought he was catching the message, when I allowed myself to be convinced we were making progress. I actually believed that he was going to move the centre of his life from the public aspect of his world to the private side.

I could almost see him kneeling before Christ, offering up his drivenness, being washed clean of all the old, terribly painful memories of a father who had flung a sense of "bumness" into his private world. How much I wanted my friend, the successful bum, to see himself a disciple called by Christ, and not one driven to achieve in order to prove something.

But it never happened. And eventually we lost contact. The last I heard, his drivenness cost him everything: family, marriage, business. For it drove him right to his grave.

MEMO TO THE DISORGANIZED

If my private world is in order, it will be because I respond to Christ's call to be a servant and form my life-purposes, my community-roles and personal identity around His fondest wishes for me.

FIVE

Living as a Called Person

SOMETIMES ONE FINDS A MOST BEAUTIFUL LINE IN AN
old book. For example, I found this one in a book
written almost eighty years ago entitled *A Casket of
Cameos*, by F. W. Boreham, in which he reflected on the
faith of Harriet Beecher Stowe's Uncle Tom (from an
even older book). Tom, an old slave, had been
wrenched from his old Kentucky home and put on a
steamship headed for unknown places. It was a terrible
moment of crisis, and Boreham observes, "Uncle Tom's
faith was staggered. It really seemed to him that, in
leaving Aunt Chloe and the children and his old
companions, he was leaving God!"

Remember, it's an old book, but there's a nugget of
truth coming.

Falling into a troubled sleep, the disoriented slave
had a dream, Boreham wrote. "He dreamed that he was
back again, and that little Eva was reading to him from
the Bible as of old. He could hear her voice: 'When thou
passest through the waters, I will be with thee; for I am
the Lord thy God, the Holy One of Israel, Thy Saviour.'"
The dream and its powerful message put Tom's heart at
rest.

A necessary rest indeed because, soon after, Tom was
suffering under the antagonisms of a sadistic master,
Simon Leg.

Boreham continues:

A little later, poor Tom was writhing under the cruel lash of his new owner. "But," says Mrs. Stowe, *"the blows fell only upon the outer man, and not, as before, on the heart.* Tom stood submissive; and yet Legree could not hide from himself the fact that his power over his victim had gone. As Tom disappeared in his cabin, and Legree wheeled his horse suddenly round, there passed through the tyrant's mind one of those vivid flashes that often send the lightning of conscience across the dark and wicked soul. He understood full well that it was God who was standing between him and Tom, and he blasphemed Him!" [1]

THE CALLED PERSON

It is this quality – the quality of an inner-directed person – for which we seek when we compare driven persons and called persons. Driven people often project a bravado of confidence as they forge ahead with their achievement-oriented life plan. But often, at the moment when it is least expected, adversities and obstructions conspire, and there can be personal collapse. Called people, on the other hand, possess strength from within, a quality of perseverance and power that are impervious to the blows from without.

You never know when you're going to bump into one of these called men or women. They can emerge from the strangest places and evince the most unique qualities. They may be the unnoticed, the unappreciated, the unsophisticated. Look again at the men Christ picked: few if any of them would have been candidates for high positions in organized religion or big business. It is not that they were unusually awkward. It is just that they appeared to be absolutely ordinary.

We have to keep reminding ourselves: No headhunter in his or her right mind would have vetted most of them for leadership in the kingdom of God. But Christ did, and that made all the difference.

The Scriptures are dotted with called men and women, of course. Mary, mother of Jesus, has to be near or at the top of the list. You wonder about what's behind the phrase, "And Mary treasured up all these things and pondered them in her heart." No need to grandstand here; no need to impress anyone.

Caleb (of Joshua and Caleb fame) sure qualifies. "I followed the Lord my God wholeheartedly," he said as he summed up his life. Or Stephen, reputed to be the first Christian martyr: "a man full of faith and the Holy Spirit." Great lines, these.

But I have to say then that when I line up all the called folk, John the Baptizer comes first. He has been an inspiration to me in the highest and, especially, the lowest moments of my life. And I have known some of the lowest of moments. On those occasions particularly, John was there with me. So let his story wash over you for a moment and see if it has the same effect it has had on me.

THE MAN WHO LOST HIS JOB

Start with courage. John the Baptizer abounded in it. When the crowds came streaming to the Jordan River valley to take his measure, John had the audacity to tell them that they ought to back off from exonerating themselves on the basis of their claim to racial or religious superiority. They should, he said, face up to their need for spiritual and moral repentance.

The baptism (usually reserved for Gentiles), he claimed, would be good for them. It would offer proof of the genuineness of their long-awaited contrition. His words must have driven the sanctimonious man in the crowd mad.

No wonder no one was ever neutral about John. The man never wasted words, never flattered a soul. You loved him or hated him. You're probably aware that one of the haters eventually removed his head. But only after John had finished his work.

Humanly speaking, John didn't have much going for him in terms of an attractive public world. We assume his parents died while he was quite young. He grew up in the desert where he partook of an austere diet and wore off-brand clothing. You can only conclude that you are watching a man with extraordinary inner strength and orientation.

John, this called man, is a marked contrast to the Old Testament's King Saul, a driven man from the start. John seems to have had from the very beginning a vivid sense of destiny, the result of a heavenly assignment that came from deep within as he immersed himself in the writings of Isaiah.

One sees the contrast between Saul and John most vividly when their personal identities and their sense of vocational security are under attack. Saul, the driven man, you will remember, reacted violently, lashing out at the younger David as he followed him all over the desert in an attempt to destroy him. And each time he encountered David, he appeared more foolish than he'd been previously.

But John is another story. Watch him when the observation is made that his popularity may be headed into serious decline. To put it another way, study John when he learns that he is losing his job.

The moment I have in mind comes after John has introduced Christ to the multitudes and they have begun to transfer their affections to this "Lamb of God" (John 1:36). It is brought to John's attention that the crowds, even some of his own disciples, are turning to Jesus, listening to His teaching and being baptized by His disciples. One gets the feeling that those who brought the news to John concerning the decline of his ratings may have anticipated (even hoped?) that they would get the chance to see John react just a bit negatively. But if that was the case, they were to be disappointed.

> A man can receive nothing, unless it has been given him from heaven. You yourselves bear me witness, that I said, "I am not the Christ," but "I have been sent before Him." He who has the bride is the bridegroom; but the friend of the bridegroom, who stands and hears him, rejoices greatly at the bridegroom's voice. And so this joy of mine has been made full. He must increase, but I must decrease. (John 3:27-30)

So what is the man saying here?

• Called People Understand Stewardship

First, John's comments begin with the principle of stewardship. Those who have instigated this conversation apparently believe that John will be rattled when he hears that his life as a crowd gatherer is over. But in fact he was anything but rattled. He seems, rather, to have been delighted.

Here's how John sees it. Having never owned the crowds in the first place, John was prepared to surrender them to Jesus if that was God's plan. That's the thinking of a steward, a key quality of a called person. The task of a steward is simply to properly manage something on behalf of the owner until the owner comes to take it back. John knew that the crowd leaving him for Christ was never his in the first place. God had placed them under his care for a period of time and now had taken them back. With John that was apparently just fine.

How different this is from the driven Saul, who assumed that he owned his throne in Israel and could do anything with it that he wished. When one owns something, it has to be held onto; it has to be protected. But John did not think that way. So when Christ came to compel the crowds, John was only too glad to hand them off and get out of the way.

John's view of stewardship presents us with an important contemporary principle. For his crowds may be our careers, our assets, our natural and spiritual gifts, our health. So – and think before answering! – are these things owned, or merely managed in the name of the One who gave them? Driven people consider them owned; called people do not. When driven people lose those things, it is a major crisis. When called people lose them, nothing of substance has changed. The private world remains the same, perhaps even stronger.

I love the words of Cardinal Danneels of Brussels:

> When I get home after a long day, I go to the chapel and pray. I say to the Lord, "There it is for today, things are finished. Now let's be serious, is this diocese mine or yours?" The Lord says, "What do you think?" I answer, "I think it's yours." "That is true," the Lord says, "it is mine." And so I say, "Listen, Lord, it is your turn to take responsibility for and direct the diocese. I'm going to sleep."[2]

• Called People Know Exactly Who They Are

A second quality of calledness is seen in John's certainty of his own identity. Let me paraphrase his remarks. You will remember that he said to his visitors, that I've told you often who I am *not*: namely, the Christ. Knowing who he was not was the beginning of knowing who he was. And John had no illusions as to his personal identity. That had already been established in his interior, private world.

By contrast, those whose private worlds are in disarray tend to get their identities confused. They can have an increasing inability to separate role from person. What they *do* is indistinguishable from who they *are*. That is why people who have wielded great power and enjoyed positions of privilege find it very difficult to give them up, and will often fight to the death to retain what they've had. It is why retirement is difficult for more than a few men and women. And it helps to explain why a mother may suffer depression when her last child has left the home. Come to think of it, I was the one who felt the depression when our kids left home. Apparently, it works either way.

We need to ponder this matter of identity carefully, for it happens to be a very contemporary subject. John could easily have taken advantage of the crowd's gullibility during the early days when he was popular. Or he could have been seduced by their applause. The fact that the masses were switching their favour from the priests of Jerusalem to him could have supercharged him with arrogance and ambition. It would have been rather simple to nod yes to questions as to whether or not he was the Messiah.

I suspect that there was a small window of time when he could have gotten away with making outlandish claims about himself. You can almost hear a man of lesser integrity than John in a moment of weakness saying, "Me, the Messiah? Well, I hadn't thought about it quite like some are saying it, but perhaps they're right, there is something kind of Messiah-like about me. Why don't I fly with this idea of Messiahship for a while and see what transpires?"

If that had been John, he probably could have pulled off the hoax for a short while. But the genuine John would not even try. His inner sphere was too well ordered for him not to have seen through the terrible implications of a misplaced identity.

If there was a moment when the crowd's praise became thunderous, the voice of God from within John was even louder. And that voice spoke more convincingly because John had first ordered his inner world out on the desert.

Don't underestimate the significance of this principle. Today in our media-fashioned world many good and talented leaders face the constant temptation to begin believing the text of their own publicity releases. And if they do, a messianic fantasy gradually infects their personalities and leadership styles. Forgetting who they are not, they begin to make dangerous assumptions about who they are. Did any of this stuff tempt the recent mayor of New York City to think that he could get the rules suspended so that he could run for a third mayoral term in a two-term system?

St. Paul offered a valuable precedent when he wrote to Timothy and recited his call from Judaism to Christian faith and apostleship: "I was the worst of sinners, he wrote; I was once a blasphemer and a persecutor and a violent man . . . the grace of our Lord was poured out on me abundantly" (1 Tim. 1:13-14). A man with a memory like that, regularly freshened, is not likely to think of himself more highly than he ought.

- **Called People Possess an Unwavering Sense of Purpose**

A third look at John's remarkable response to his interrogators will reveal that the prophet from the desert also understood the purpose of his activity as forerunner to Christ. And this is another dimension of calledness. To those who questioned him regarding his feelings about the growing popularity of the Man from Nazareth, he likened his purpose to that of the best man at a wedding: "He who has the bride is the bridegroom; but the friend [that's John] of the bridegroom, who stands and hears him, rejoices greatly because of the bridegroom's voice" (John 3:29). The purpose of the best man is simply to stand with the groom, to make sure that all attention is riveted upon him. The best man would be a fool if in the middle of the wedding processional he suddenly turned to the wedding guests and began to sing a song or engage in a humorous monologue. The best man has fulfilled his purpose most admirably when he draws no attention to himself but focuses all attention upon the bride and groom.

And that is what John did. If Jesus Christ was the groom, to use John's metaphor, then the Baptizer was committed to being best man and *nothing* else. That was the purpose that flowed from his call, and he had no desire to aspire to anything beyond. Thus to see the crowd headed toward Christ was all the affirmation John needed; his purpose had been fulfilled. But only called people like this man can relax under such circumstances.

I love Robert Browning's lines in his poem, "Bishop Bloughram's Apology:"

In everyman's career are certain points
Whereon he dares not be indifferent;
The world detects him clearly, if he dare,
As baffled at the game and losing life.

Among the things we can say about John is this: He was never baffled, and he never lost life. Hard to do if your purpose is lofty and imaginative, if it calls from you every ounce of moral and spiritual energy you have, if it is bigger than you are.

When the 9/11 catastrophe took New York's Trade Towers down, my wife, Gail, and I headed for Ground

Zero to contribute our energies to the work of the Salvation Army. During that first week when all seemed so chaotic, we were part of the thousands of workers and their relief supports who attacked the rubble in hopes that we would find trapped people still alive.

By the hour I worked as part of a team that brought everything from cold water to fresh boots to the men and women who formed the bucket brigades intent on getting to anyone who had survived. Occasionally, we would hear the signal that meant "Silence" as the suspicion arose that a voice or tapping was heard underneath the concrete and steel.

Late one night I stood in a circle of fire-fighters who had been working 24/7, refusing to rest.

"Don't you think you'd profit from a few hours away from this place?" I asked.

"Not a chance," their leader said. "We've got brothers in that pile, and they may be waiting for us."

It was moments like this that would cause me to occasionally find Gail at the station where she was dispensing aid, walk off to a corner with her, take her into my arms, and whisper, "I was made for this!"

Now I have a slight, momentary sense of how the great saints – John the Baptizer included – must have continually felt as they lived down through the centuries, caught up in a lofty sense of purpose.

- **Called People Practice Unswerving Commitment**

Finally, John, as a called man, also understood that some things need to be released. Mothers know they must eventually release their children to a more independent life. Mentors know they must release their protégés at an appropriate moment.

John's comment, "He must increase, but I must decrease" (John 3:30), spoken to those who had queried him about his attitude, illustrates the principle of planned released. A called person – because he is a steward, because he knows who he is, because he is purposeful – anticipates the day when it is time to step back and let go. In this case it was a crowd, a temporary reputation, and a bevy of disciples that had to be released to Jesus' influence.

No driven person could ever say what John said, because driven people have to keep gaining more and more attention, more and more power, more and more material assets. They have to hold on; they cannot let go. Too much of themselves is wound up in what they are doing.

Occasionally we hear the story of an organizational leader who, having given powerful leadership to an institution, comes toward the end of his working life and keeps holding on to leadership long after he should have let it pass into the hands of someone in a younger generation. Or he ensures that the leadership passes into the hands of a son or a daughter so that he can maintain his influence.

Somewhere in my library is a book in which the story is told of an English headmaster who was appointed when he was forty-five years of age. His first act was to write himself a letter to be opened on his sixty-fifth birthday. In it he wrote (and I paraphrase), "Today you are sixty-five, and it is time to give the task of being headmaster over to a younger person. You will tell yourself that there is no one who can replace you; that the school cannot do without you. But don't believe this self-aggrandizing propaganda."

Sure enough, when he turned sixty-five and opened the letter, he found that he entertained those exact feelings about his indispensability. But he took his own advice and released the leadership to another. Which is exactly what John did.

It is these kinds of qualities – John's sense of stewardship, his awareness of his identity, his perspective about his role, and his commitment to the principle of release – that mark a called person. And they are the characteristics of a person who builds first in the interior or private world so that out of it will flow fountains of life.

How totally different were the lives of Saul the king and John the Baptizer. The one sought to defend a golden cage, and lost; the other was pleased with a place in the desert and a chance to serve, and won.

You sense a maturity in John's thinking that is uncommon. There's a peacefulness about him. This is not a rattled man whose sense of well-being craters when his public world changes.

There's a quality of joy that ought not to be confused with the modern-day version of happiness – a state of feelings dependent upon everything turning out all right. When others thought that John might be worried about ending up as a failure, they discovered that he actually was quite satisfied, in spite of the fact that his audiences were leaving him. Some folk in John's generation might not have thought so, but John had such an assurance because his evaluations were based first on his private world, where real values can be fully formed in concert with God.

John is in fact the quintessential called man. He illustrates what Stowe meant when she wrote that Simon Legree's blows fell only upon Uncle Tom's outer man, but not upon his heart. Something stood between John and the public evidence that he may have been a failure. It was the unquestioned reality of God's call, which John had heard in that private world of his. And that voice was louder than any other sound. It came from a quiet place of order.

THE ROAD TO CALLEDNESS

As one looks with admiration at John the Baptizer, the obvious question is, How did he get that way? What was the source of this determination, this stamina, this unswerving ability to look at events in a totally different way than others did? A quick overview of John's background offers some insights into the structure and substance of his inner life.

If there is one thing that begins to explain John, it has to be the kind of parents he had, who shaped him in his earliest days. He had good genes, physically and spiritually.

It is clear from Scripture that Zacharias and Elizabeth were godly people with extraordinary sensitivity to John's call. It had been revealed to them through various angelic visions. And they in turn from the earliest days began to pump that destiny into John's soul. We have little indication of John's family life after he was born, but we do know that his parents were marked with an extraordinary depth of integrity, godliness, and perseverance.

John's parents must have died when he was still a very young man. How he handled the loss we do not know. But when the Scripture next highlights John, he is living alone in the desert, separate from the society to which he would later speak as a prophet.

> In the fifteenth year of the reign of Tiberius Caesar, when Pontius Pilate was governor of Judea, and Herod was tetrarch of Galilee, and his brother Philip was tetrarch of the region of Ituraea and Trachonitis, and Lysanias was tetrarch of Abilene, in the high priesthood of Annas and Caiaphas, the word of God came to John, the son of Zacharias, in the wilderness. And he came into all the district around the Jordan,

preaching a baptism of repentance for the forgiveness of sins. (Luke 3:1-3)

These words contain an intriguing insight. Caesar, we're reminded, was in Rome doing whatever important things Caesars do. Annas and Caiaphas, major-league priests, were in the Jerusalem temple promoting organized religion. And various other political personalities were going and coming in public places, participating in seemingly newsworthy events. Their worlds were the impressive public worlds of power, notoriety, and human connection.

Then this: But *the word of God came to John,* an insignificant man in the most insignificant of places: a desert. Why John? And why a desert? Think about it!

I am reminded of Herbert Butterfield's words, which have always humbled me:

> Both in history and in life it is a phenomenon by no means rare to meet with comparatively unlettered people who seem to have struck profound spiritual depths . . . while there are many highly educated people of whom one feels that they are performing clever antics with their minds to cover a gaping hollowness that lies within.[3]

So why John? First answer: Only God knows. Beyond that one simply has to say because John responded. The call demanded submission to God's ways, God's methods, and God's criteria for success. And John was willing to accept those terms no matter what the cost to him in pain or loneliness.

Why a desert? Perhaps because in deserts people can hear and brood upon things not easily heard or thought about in busy cities, where people are usually hurried, surrounded by noise, and steeped in self-importance. Sometimes in cities the shrillness of the public life is so great that the whispering voice of God cannot be heard. And sometimes in cities, people are too proud to listen to God amid all of their steel and concrete skyscrapers, their colourful theatres, or their incredible temples.

God drew John into the desert where He could speak to him. And when He got him there He began to stamp impressions onto John's inner world that gave the son of Zacharias a totally different perspective on his times. There in the desert he gained a new view of religion, of right and wrong, of God's purposes for history. And there he developed a special sensitivity and courage that would prepare him for his most extraordinary task: introducing his generation to the Christ. His private world was under construction – in the desert.

The word of God came to John in the desert. Such a strange place for God to speak. What can one learn in deserts? I am inclined to forsake deserts, to detour around them whenever possible. To me, deserts mean pain, isolation, and suffering. And no one cares for any of that. Deserts are hard places in which to live, physically or spiritually. But the fact is unavoidable: The greatest lessons are potentially learned in deserts if one, in the midst of struggle, listens for God's call.

In deserts, one learns about dryness, because deserts are dry. John would learn not only to cope with the dryness of the desert, but it doubtless taught him to appreciate the aridity of the spirits of the people to whom he'd speak at the Jordan.

In the desert a person learns dependence upon God. Life in the wilderness, as the Hebrews had found out centuries before, cannot be sustained without the benevolence of a merciful God. Only a person who has suffered desert-like hardship knows what it is like to totally cast himself upon God because there is nothing else left.

There is a slightly brighter side to deserts, however. Wilderness provides a place where one is free to think, to plan, to prepare. And then at an appointed time, like

John, he comes charging out of the dry land with a message, something to say that will expose hypocrisy and superficiality. Issues are addressed that cut through to the bottomless depths of the human spirit. And an age of people is introduced to the Christ of God.

In the desert a person can be called. As John stood up first to his critics and then to the furiously defensive Herod, whose immoral life the prophet rebuked, he began to reveal that special quality of calledness. You can see it in his serenity in the midst of his prophetic performance. Something special within was operating, providing him with an independent base of judgement and wisdom. Few could withstand his message.

What was the makeup of that private world that was formed in the desert? Frankly, the biblical writers do not give us much of an answer. We are simply treated to the evidence of an ordered inner life. John is a prototype of the product we are looking for. In a public world where all seems chaotic and disordered, he moves with assurance and certitude.

Have Saul, John, and my friend the "successful bum" taught us anything? I think their message is plain. Look inside, they say. What makes you tick? Why are you doing all of that? What do you hope to gain as a result? And what would be your reaction if it were all taken away?

I look inside my private world and discover that almost every day I have to wrestle with whether I will be a Saul or a John. I have lived in a competitive world where achievement is almost everything. Now as I journey through my sixties, the challenge has morphed a bit: how to back out of organizational leadership and influence, gracefully turn it over to another generation, and embrace a quieter (and far more sane, actually) role: being a mentor, a cheerleader, an encourager to the young.

This may sound sort of noble, but it's not always that simple. I always enjoyed being in charge, more or less. I could still find it easy to join Saul, to be driven to hold on, to protect, to dominate. And I might even find myself doing those sorts of things while telling myself that I was doing God's work. But as John did, I have concluded that it's time to practice the principle of release and go on to other things. As Henri Nouwen eloquently put it: to embrace littleness, hiddenness, and powerlessness. Frankly, I'd rather hug other things, but this is the way of the cross, the way of the called person.

Sector Two

MEMO TO THE DISORGANIZED

If my private world is in order, it will be because I have made daily determination to see time as God's gift and worthy of careful investment.

SIX

Has Anyone Seen My Time?
I've Misplaced It!

I HAD JUST FINISHED A LECTURE TO A GROUP OF PASTORS in which I mentioned a number of books I'd recently read. When the talk was finished, a young pastor asked, "Where do you find the time to read all of those books? When I entered the pastorate, I was sure I was going to be able to do that kind of reading too. But I haven't read anything for weeks now. I'm just too swamped!"

We talked for a short while about the discipline of reading, and the conversation began to branch out into other aspects of his personal life. He shared his guilt about his spiritual exercises; they were almost nonexistent. He admitted that it had been a long time since he had spent anything approaching quality time with his wife. He bemoaned the fact that his sermons were usually substandard by his own evaluation. And at the conclusion of our conversation, he conceded that his failure even to read a book was merely the hint of an even bigger struggle. "Frankly," he said, "I'm totally disorganized. I'm not getting anything of consequence done."

I am very sympathetic with this young man and his admission. There was a time in my own life when I could have said the same thing. And I don't think either one of us would have found ourselves alone if our colleagues at that lecture had been honest. The world is full of disorganized people who have lost control of their time.

Ours can be a wordy religion, meaning that one can go a long way, impress a lot of people, simply through a facility with words. So it becomes easy to make promises, verbalize intentions, express one's convictions with seeming passion. But behind the talk can be a lot of wasted time and energy. And so we sometimes meet people who do not keep their promises, finish what they start, or back up their verbal intensity with dependable performance. Reason: They do not know how to match their time with appropriate performance.

William Barclay, commenting upon the undisciplined life of Samuel Taylor Coleridge, wrote:

> Coleridge is the supreme tragedy of indiscipline. Never did so great a mind produce so little. He left Cambridge University to join the army; he left the army because he could not rub down a horse; he returned to Oxford and left without a degree. He began a paper called The Watchman, which lived for ten numbers and then died. It has been said of him: "He lost himself in visions of work to be done, that always remained to be done. Coleridge had every poetic gift but one – the gift of sustained and concentrated effort." In his head and in his mind he had all kinds of books, as he said, himself, "completed save for transcription. I am on the even," he says, "of sending to the press two octavo volumes." But the books were never composed outside Coleridge's mind, because he would not face the discipline of sitting down to write them out. No one ever reached any eminence, and no one having reached it ever maintained it, without discipline.[1]

Coleridge was living proof that a man or woman may be multitalented, possess enormous intelligence and remarkable communicative gifts, and yet end up squandering it all because of an inability to seize control of time. Coleridge's futile pursuits in the literary world are mirrored by some whose vocation is in the home, in the church, or at the office.

None of us, I am sure, wants to come to the end of his life and look back with regrets on things that could have been accomplished but were not, as happened to Coleridge. But to prevent that from happening, it is necessary to understand how we can command the time God has given to us.

SYMPTOMS OF DISORGANIZATION

The first step we may have to take is that of a ruthless self-appraisal about our habits of time use. Are we actually disorganized or not? Let us consider the traits of a disorganized life. Some of these symptoms may seem a bit ridiculous, even petty. But they are usually part of a larger picture that all fits together. Let me suggest a handful of sample symptoms.

When I am slipping into a state of disorganization, for example, I know it because my desk takes on a cluttered appearance. The same thing happens to the top of my bedroom dresser. In fact almost every horizontal surface in the path of my daily travel becomes littered with papers, memos to which I have not responded, and bits of tasks that are unfinished. I can see some spouse saying, "Here, read this; he's been in your office lately." But my desk can be another's kitchen counter, work bench, or basement workroom. The same principle applies.

The symptoms of disorganization tend to show themselves in the condition of my car. It becomes dirty inside and out. I lose track of its maintenance schedule, and I find that I am pressing deadlines for things like changing snow tires and getting the annual safety sticker.

When disorganization takes over, I become aware of a diminution in my self-esteem. I feel the slightest tinge of paranoia, a low-level fear that people are going to discover they are not getting their money's worth out of my labour, that they are going to come to the conclusion that I am not half the man they thought I was.

I know I'm disorganized when there are a series of forgotten appointments, telephone messages to which I have failed to respond, and deadlines I have begun to miss. The day becomes filled with broken commitments and lame excuses. (I must be careful to say, incidentally, that I am not thinking of times when events beyond my control have conspired to derail even the best intentions. All of us have those kinds of days, even the most organized of us.)

If I am disorganized, I tend to invest my energies in unproductive tasks. I actually find myself doing small and boring things just to get something accomplished. There is a tendency toward daydreaming, an avoidance of decisions that have to be made, and procrastination. Disorganization begins to affect every part of my will to work steadily and excellently.

Disorganized people feel poor about their work. What they manage to finish they do not like. They find it very hard to accept the compliments of others. In the secrecy of their hearts they know that they have turned in a second-best job.

I have more than once driven home from Sunday morning worship services where I have preached in this sort of mood. And as I drove, I found myself pounding the steering wheel in frustration because I knew that I could have preached better if I had used my time during the week more effectively in study and preparation.

Disorganized Christians rarely enjoy intimacy with God. They certainly have intentions of pursuing that camaraderie, but it never quite gets established. No one

---

has to tell them that time must be set aside for the purpose of Bible study and reflection, for intercession, for worship. They know all of that. They simply are not doing it. They excuse themselves, saying there is no time, but within their private worlds they know it is more a matter of organization and personal will than anything else.

If I am in a state of disorganization, the quality of my personal relationships usually reveals it. The days pass without a significant conversation with my son or daughter. My wife and I will be in contact, but our conversations may be shallow, devoid of self-revelation, and unaffirming. I may become irritable, resenting any attempt on her part to call to my attention things I have left undone or people I appear to have let down.

The fact of the matter is that when we are disorganized in our control of time, we just don't like ourselves, our jobs, or much else about our worlds. And it is difficult to break the destructive pattern that settles in.

This terrible habit pattern of disorganization must be broken, or our private worlds will fall quickly into total disorder. We must resolve to seize control of our time.

Psychologists can suggest many reasons for people's being disorganized, and it is helpful to think some of these through. There is a large body of helpful literature available on the subject of time management and organization. But beneath the gimmicks and tricks of organization are some fundamental principles that have to be seriously considered by any person seeking an ordering of the private world. Putting these principles into practice will be a challenge for some men and women who have ignored the importance of controlling their time.

BUDGETING TIME

The central principle of all personal organization of time is simple: Time must be budgeted!

Most of us learned this about money a long time ago. When we discovered that we rarely had enough money to do all the things we wanted to do with it, we found it prudent to sit down and think through our financial priorities.

With money, the priorities were obvious. Since my wife and I are committed to God's plan of stewardship, our first financial priority has always been our tithe and offerings. Then the fixed expenditures of food, house, utilities, books (both of us insist that books are a fixed expenditure), and so on have been set aside in amounts that we have learned to anticipate.

Only after we have budgeted these amounts of money for the necessities have we ventured into the discretionary side of the budget, namely those things that are more wants than needs. Here we may be talking about a meal out at a favourite restaurant, an appliance that makes life a bit easier, or a particularly attractive winter coat.

When men and women do not understand the difference between the fixed and the discretionary aspects of their financial lives, they usually end up in debt, which is the financial version of disorganization.

When money is limited, one budgets. And when time is in limited supply, the same principle holds. The disorganized person must have a budgeting perspective. And that means determining the difference between the fixed – what one must do – and the discretionary – what one would *like* to do.

These were the items I raised when my young pastor friend came to talk about why he felt so unproductive.

He was surprised when I told him that we were talking about one of my own daily battles.

"Gordon," he said, "you don't convey the impression that time is ever out of your control."

I protested, "I sometimes wonder if I've ever got any of it under control." All of those symptoms of the disorganized life were at one time or another my symptoms, but I had made a decision (actually on more than one occasion) that I was not going to live that way for one more minute than I had to.

THE LORD OF TIME

My young pastor friend was obviously hoping I would share with him a few of the insights that have challenged me to order my private world in the area of time use. If he thought I had a bag of answers that would make it easy, he was to be disappointed. As our conversation continued, I suggested that he take a hard look at one Person who never seems to have wasted a moment.

When I look into the Bible, I am deeply impressed with the practical lessons on organization that one can learn from the life and work of Jesus Christ. All four Gospel writers present to us a picture of Jesus under constant pressure, as He was pursued by friend and enemy alike. His every word was monitored, every action was analyzed, every gesture was commented upon. Essentially, Jesus had no private life to speak of.

I have tried to imagine our Lord in today's world. Would He carry a pager or a cell phone? Which would He choose: a Palm Pilot or a HandSpring? Would He fly, drive, or take the train? Would He be drawn to direct-mail campaigns? How would He handle the huge number of relationships that modern technology has made it possible for us to maintain? How would He fit in to a time where a word spoken can be flashed around the world in seconds to become headlines for the next morning's paper?

Although His everyday world was on a much smaller scale, it would appear that He lived with very much the same sort of intrusions and demands with which we are familiar. But one never gets the feeling when studying the life of Christ that He ever hurried, that He ever had to play "catch-up," or that He was ever taken by surprise. Not only was He adept at handling His public time without an appointments secretary, but He also managed adequate amounts of time alone for the purpose of prayer and meditation, and for being with the few He had gathered around Him for the purpose of discipleship. Again, all this was made possible because He had brought His time under control.

It is worth taking time to ask how our Lord's command of time is demonstrated. What caused Him to be such an organized person?

The first thing that impresses me is that Jesus clearly understood His mission. He had an overarching task to perform, and He measured His use of time against that sense of mission. This is quite apparent during His final walk toward Jerusalem, where He would be crucified. As Jesus approached Jericho, Luke wrote (chapter 18), His ears picked up the shrill voice of a blind man and He stopped, much to the consternation of both His friends and critics. They were irritated that Jesus did not appreciate that Jerusalem was still six or seven hours away, and that they would like to get there to achieve their purpose, the celebration of Passover.

And indeed they had a point: the purpose of Christ was merely to reach Jerusalem in time for a religious celebration. But as we soon learn, that was not Jesus' prime mission. Touching broken people like the blind man was a more significant matter, important enough for Jesus to invest His time.

Not long after the first encounter, Jesus stopped once again, this time under the branch of a tree to call down Zacchaeus, a well-known tax collector. It was the Lord's idea that the two get together for a conversation at Zacchaeus's house. Once again the crowd surrounding Jesus was incensed, first because the trip to Jerusalem was again interrupted, and second because of Zacchaeus's reputation.

From where they were standing, it appeared that Jesus was misusing His time. From where Jesus was standing, however, the time was well spent, for it fit the criteria of His mission.

Luke recorded the words of Jesus about this very fact: "The Son of Man has come to seek and save that which was lost" (Luke 19:10). The disciples had a difficult time understanding this, and Jesus had to constantly confront them with the specific facts of His mission. Until they owned that mission, they would never understand how and with what criteria He organized His time.

A second insight into Jesus' personal organization of time is that He understood His own limits. When Jesus came to earth as the incarnate Son of God, He set aside certain of His rights as the Prince of Heaven and accepted, for a time, certain human limitations in order to fully identify with us. He shared our limitations but coped with them effectively – just as we must.

We dare not minimize the fact that Jesus sought time in solitude with the heavenly Father before every important decision and action during His public ministry.

There are thirty years of virtual silence before Jesus went public with His mission. Only when we are treated to an audience with Christ in eternity will we fully understand the importance of those three decades. At best, we can now conclude that they were a significant time of preparation. It is impressive to realize that there were thirty years of relative obscurity and privacy in preparation for three years of important activity.

We should not be surprised, then, that Moses spent forty years in the desert before confronting Pharaoh. Paul spent an extensive amount of time in the desert listening to God before assuming apostolic duties. And the experience of these men was not exceptional.

Just before Jesus assumed public ministry, He spent forty days in the wilderness communing with the Father. Don't forget the night spent in prayer before the choosing of the twelve. There was an early-morning vigil on the mountainside the day after a busy time in Capernaum. And of course there was withdrawal to the Mount of Transfiguration to prepare for the final trek to Jerusalem. Finally, there was Gethsemane.

Jesus knew His limits well. Strange as it may seem, He knew what we conveniently forget: that time must be properly budgeted for the gathering of inner strength and resolve in order to compensate for one's weaknesses when spiritual warfare begins. Such private moments were a fixed item on Jesus' time budget because He knew His limits. And it was very hard even for those closest to Him to fully appreciate this.

I think Jesus included a third important element in His strategy of time budgeting, for He set time aside for the training of the Twelve. With a world of millions to reach, Jesus budgeted the majority of His time to be with just a few simple men.

Prime time was invested in taking them through the Scriptures and sharing His heavenly insights. Key moments were spent sharing ministry with individuals and permitting them to watch every action and hear every word. Special days were set aside to explain to them the deeper meanings of His talks to the crowds. And valuable hours were seized in order to debrief them when they returned from assignments, to rebuke them when they failed, and to affirm them when they succeeded.

We might have been tempted to ask more than once why Jesus was spending so much valuable time with a group of simple-minded men when He could have taught men who could have intellectually appreciated His theological expertise. But Jesus was aware of where true importance lies, where the priorities are. And where your priorities are, there your time will be.

For reasons like these, Jesus was never to be caught short on time. Because He knew His sense of mission, because He was spiritually sharpened by moments alone with the Father, and because He knew who the men were that would perpetuate His mission long after He ascended into heaven, it was never difficult for Him to say a firm no to invitations and demands that might have looked good or acceptable to us.

There came a time in my own life when my study of Jesus made me deeply desire this capacity. I wanted to make sound decisions about the budgeting of my time, and I wanted to be free of that frantic pitch of daily life in which one is always playing catch-up. Was it possible? Not the way I was going!

The young pastor who had come to me at the end of my lecture remained very interested. I suggested that we get together on another day. Perhaps there would be some practical things I could share with him. But I would have to be brutally honest with him. I learned most of them the hard way.

MEMO TO THE DISORGANIZED

If my private world is in order, it is because I have begun to "seal" the time-leaks and allocate my productive hours in light of my capabilities, my limits and my priorities.

SEVEN

Recapturing My Time

THE YOUNG PASTOR AND I WERE TO RESUME OUR conversation some days later. In the interim I began gathering thoughts about what I had learned over the past few years that had helped me begin getting my own life together in this area. What had I learned through the experience of failure, and what had I learned in talking with others in the same way that this young man was coming to talk with me?

The more I looked at the lessons learned, the more I realized how important it is to gain control of time as early in life as possible. Putting them down on paper, I discovered that there were only a few basic principles. But until those were mastered, the time issue would always be big and potentially discouraging. What I found myself writing down in preparation for my next conversation was something I came to call "MacDonald's Laws of Unmanaged Time." Here is what I collected.

MACDONALD'S LAWS OF UNMANAGED TIME

Law #1: Unmanaged Time Flows Toward My Weaknesses

Because I had not adequately defined a sense of mission in the early days of my work, and because I had not been ruthless enough with my weaknesses, I found that I normally invested inordinately large amounts of time doing things I was not good at, while the tasks I should have been able to do with excellence and effectiveness were preempted.

I know many Christian leaders who feel that they spend up to 60 percent of their time (perhaps a lot more, actually) doing things at which they are second best. For example, I am an idea person. I am comfortable thinking, as they say, outside the box; I am not disturbed by ambiguity; I have a nose for patterns and trend-lines. Beyond that, I enjoy challenging the status quo. That sort of strength gets fleshed out as a preacher, a teacher, and a consultant of sorts. It offers a form of organizational leadership as a visionary – someone who sees possibilities a second or two before others might see them.

But this capability demands large blocks of time for reading, studying, and reflecting. In the earlier days of Polaroid, when Dr. Edwin Land, its founder, was in his prime, the Polaroid people saw that he could be of supreme value to the company if he was excused from running the company on a day-to-day basis and given a research lab where he could use his mighty gift to come up with new concepts that would result in new products. It was a splendid idea, and everyone won as a result.

The churches I have pastored rarely saw that there might be a similar value – as an idea person – in me so they tended to insist that I invest a lot of my time doing things at which I am less than best: namely people management and administration. So I did it, made a choice to enjoy it, but rarely felt satisfied that I was giving the organization my best.

So why did I spend almost 75 percent of my available time trying to administrate and relatively little time studying and preparing to preach good sermons when I was younger? Because unseized time will flow in the direction of one's relative weakness. Since I knew I could preach an acceptable sermon with a minimum of preparation, I was actually doing less than my best in the pulpit. That is what happens when one does not evaluate this matter and do something drastic about it.

So I did the drastic thing. I sought the aid of a few sensitive men who cared enough to help me face what was happening and to show me how I might be squandering my potential. With their help I made a decision to delegate the administration of our congregation's ministry to a competent administrative pastor. It was not easy at first because I was in the habit of offering an opinion on every decision. Now I had to back off and leave that in someone else's hands. But it worked! And when I was able to fully trust our administrative pastor (which I soon found easy to do), I was able to redirect a great amount of energy into things that, God willing, I am most likely to do well.

I can almost hear someone say, "That's fine if the money is available to hire someone to compensate for my weaknesses." And perhaps in some cases the only help these comments may offer is to make us realize *why* we are frustrated when time seems to escape us. But I must add that it may be more possible than we realize to find creative ways to share tasks with others. First, we must sit ourselves down and consider who is best at doing what? This applies in the home, in the office, and in the church.

Law #2: Unmanaged Time Comes Under the Influence of Dominant People in My World

A famous "spiritual law" states that "God loves you and has a plan for your life." Men and women who do not have control of their time discover that the same can be said about dominating people.

Because they have not set up their own time budgets, people succumbing to this law find that others enter their worlds and press agendas and priorities upon them. As a young pastor I discovered that because my time was not fully organized, I was at the mercy of anyone who had a notion to visit, took me to coffee, or wanted my attendance at a committee meeting. Since my calendar was disorganized, how could I say no? Especially when, as a young man, I was eager to please people.

Not only was I deprived of my best time due to this lack of organization, but my family was often cheated out of precious hours that I should have given them. And so it continued. Strong people in my world controlled my time better than I did because I had not taken the initiative to command the time before they got to me. This sometimes led to resentment toward them and disrespect toward myself. Not a good way to live.

Law #3: Unmanaged Time Surrenders to the Demands of All Emergencies

Charles Hummel writing years ago in a small and classic booklet said it best: We are governed by the tyranny of the urgent. Those of us with any sort of responsibility for leadership in vocation, in the home, or in our faith will find ourselves continually

---

surrounded by events that cry out for immediate attention.

One summer, years ago, when our associate pastor and I were both on vacation, one of our staff members took a phone call from a church member who wanted me to preside at the funeral of a distant relative of his. When told that I was away for the month, he asked for my associate and was disappointed to discover that he was also gone. He was offered the services of one of the other pastors on the staff, but he refused, saying, "No, I won't go any lower than number two."

His thinking was the sort that creates urgent situations for leaders. Everyone would like the attention of the number-one person. Every committee and board would like the number-one person to attend their meetings, even if they do not always wish to hear his opinions. Most people in any sort of trouble would like the immediate response of the number-one leader.

One Saturday afternoon the phone rang in our home, and when I answered, the woman's voice at the other end of the line sounded quite upset. "I've got to see you right away," she said. When I learned her name, I quickly realized that I had never met this person before and that she had rarely ever visited our church.

"What is the reason that we have to visit right now?" I asked. It was an important question, one of several I've learned through experience to ask. Had this been many years ago when I was young, I would have responded immediately to her sense of emergency and arranged to meet her in ten minutes at my office, even if I had previously hoped to be with the family or involved with study.

"My marriage is breaking up," she responded. I then asked, "When did you become aware that it was going to break up?"

She answered, "Last Tuesday." I asked another question. "How long do you think the process of breaking up has been going on?" Her next comment was unforgettable.

"Oh, it's been coming for five years." I managed to stifle my real reaction and said, "Since you've seen this coming for almost five years, and since you knew it was going to happen since last Tuesday, why is it important to visit with me right at this moment? I need to know that."

She answered, "Oh, I had some free time this afternoon and just thought it might be a good time to get together with you."

Law number three would usually mean that I would have surrendered to her desire to see me immediately. But by this point in my life, most of my time was accounted for; so I said, "I can understand why you think you have a serious problem. Now I'm going to be very candid with you. I have to preach three times tomorrow morning, and frankly my mind is preoccupied with that responsibility. Since you've been living with this situation for several years now, and since you've had several days to think about your situation, I'm going to propose that you call me on Monday morning when we can arrange a time where my mind is in much better shape. I want to be able to give you the utmost in concentration. But that's probably not possible this afternoon. How does that sound?"

She thought it was a terrific idea and could see why I would suggest that sort of plan. Both of us hung up reasonably happy: she, knowing she would eventually get to talk to me; me, because I had reserved my time for the matter that was most important on that Saturday afternoon. A seemingly urgent thing had not broken through the time budget. Not everything that cries the loudest is the most urgent thing.

In his spiritual autobiography (one of my favourites), *While It Is Day,* Elton Trueblood wrote:

> A public man, though he is necessarily available at many times, must learn to hide. If he is always available, he is not worth enough when he is available. I once wrote a chapter in the Cincinnati Union Station, but that was itself a form of hiding because nobody knew who the man with the writing pad was. Consequently nobody approached me during five wonderful hours until the departure of the next train to Richmond. *We must use the time which we have because even at best there is never enough.* [italics added][1]

Trueblood's comments, seemingly dated, are as fresh today as the moment he wrote them years ago.

Law #4: Unmanaged Time Gets Invested in Things That Gain Public Acclamation

In other words, we are more likely to give our unbudgeted time to events that will bring the most immediate and greatest praise.

When Gail and I were first married, we found that we could attract a lot of invitations to banquets and meetings of various sorts if we were willing to sing solos and duets. It was nice to receive the warm applause and gain the popularity. But the performance of music was not our call or our priority. Preaching and pastoral care were. Unfortunately, young preachers were not (and rarely are) in great demand, and the temptation was to do anything that would make us attractive to people.

We had to make a critical decision. Would we involve our time in doing what people most liked for us to do? Or would we buckle down and give our attention to what was most important: learning the ways of preaching and counselling? Fortunately, we chose to avoid the seduction of the former and embrace the latter. It paid off.

We have had to make choices like that throughout our married life. And more than once I have made the wrong choice. There was a time when it seemed glamorous to fly across the country to speak at a banquet. But it was a poor use of time. The old comment "A sermon is something I'd go across the country to preach but not across the street to hear" is too close to the truth to be comfortable. It once seemed enchanting to be at the head table of some politician's prayer breakfast or to be interviewed on a Christian radio program, but it may not have been a high priority use of time.

Thus, the laws of unmanaged time come back to haunt the disorganized person again and again, until he decides to gain the initiative before everyone and every event does it for him.

RECAPTURING LOST TIME

In gathering material for that upcoming conversation with the young pastor, I looked back on my own experience, trying to identify the principles that, when implemented, brought some order into my private world. And when I thought hard about the process that I had come through, I found that I was able to come up with three ways of successfully recapturing time.

1. I Must Know My Rhythms of Maximum Effectiveness. A careful study of my work habits has revealed to me an important insight. There are various tasks I accomplish best at certain times and under certain conditions.

For example, I do not study effectively for Sunday sermons during the early days of the week. Two hours of study on Monday are relatively worthless, while one hour (and hopefully a lot more) on Thursday or Friday is almost priceless. I simply concentrate better. On the other hand, I am at my best with people in the early days of a week when the tension of anticipated preaching has not yet grabbed my mind. I tend to diminish in effectiveness with people later in the week when I become preoccupied with Sunday's pulpit experience.

I can fine-tune that observation even further. What study time I do take is best taken early in the morning, when I have reasonable amounts of unbroken solitude. And "people time" for me is best taken in the afternoon, when I feel reflective and insightful.

Learning about my rhythms has taught me to reserve study time for the last half of the week and to plan time with people and committees as much as possible in the first part of the week. In this way, my time budget reflects and uses the rhythms of my life.

I have also taken notice of the fact that I am a morning person. I can rise early and be quite alert if I have gone to bed at a reasonable hour the night before. So it is important to me to maintain a fairly standard bedtime. We enforced that principle with our children when they were young. I don't know why it never dawned upon us that a standard bedtime as much as possible was probably a wise thing for us as adults. And when I finally saw this, I tried to go to bed at the same time each night.

After reading an article by a specialist on the subject of sleep, I began to experiment to find out how much sleep I needed. The writer suggested that one can determine his sleep requirements by setting his alarm for a certain hour and rising at that time for three mornings in a row. Then the alarm should be set ten minutes earlier for the next three days. By so continuing in three-day increments, setting the alarm back ten minutes in each period, one will finally come to a natural fatigue point, where throughout the following day he does not feel properly rested. I tried it, found I could rise much earlier than I had thought, and it added almost two full hours – valuable hours – to my day.

So there are weekly rhythms, daily rhythms, and annual rhythms. I found that there were certain months of the year when I was apt to face abnormal emotional fatigue, times when part of me wanted to run from people and from responsibility. I had to face up to that.

On the other hand, I saw that there were times in the year when I had to be relatively stronger as a Christian leader because many people around me were living with too much fatigue and pressure. The months of February and March are times like that, when all of us in New England fight the effects of a long winter and tend toward irritability and a critical spirit. I have learned to prepare myself to be an extra special encouragement to others during those times. And when spring comes and people feel revitalized, then I can enjoy my own private time of letdown. Knowing those things were likely to happen was a great help to me. I could plan for them.

I have learned that the summer months are a fine time for extra reading and for spiritually preparing myself for the coming year. But during January through March, for reasons I have just mentioned, I plan to be with people much of the time, because the counselling schedule is likely to jump dramatically. All of my books have been written in the summer months; there is no way they could have been done in winter.

Knowing my rhythms, I am not surprised when I feel inwardly empty after a period of heavy speaking and teaching. I cannot live day after day above the emotional line without coming to a moment when I must dip just a bit beneath the line of emotional normalcy to regather strength that has been lost. Thus I learned as a pastor that it was wise not to make important decisions on a Monday after a day of preaching several sermons. And if I had pushed hard day after day during a holiday season, it was wise for me to plan a short comedown period when it was all over.

I prize a segment in a letter that William Booth, founder of the Salvation Army, once received from his wife when he was on an extensive trip.

> Your Tuesday's notes arrived safe, and I was rejoiced to hear of the continued prosperity of the work, though sorry you were so worn out; I fear the effect of all this excitement and exertion upon your health, and though I would not hinder your usefulness, I would caution you against an injudicious prodigality of your strength.

> Remember a long life of steady, consistent, holy labour will produce twice as much fruit as one shortened and destroyed by spasmodic and extravagant exertions; be careful and sparing of your strength when and where exertion is unnecessary.[2]

2. *I Must Have Thoughtful Criteria for Choosing How to Use My Time.* Years ago my father suggested that one of the great tests of human character is found in making critical choices of selection and rejection amidst all of the opportunities that lurk in life's path. "Your challenge," he told me, "will not be in separating out the good from the bad, but in grabbing the best out of all the possible good." He was absolutely correct. I did indeed have to learn, sometimes the hard way, that I had to say no to things I really wanted to do in order to say yes to the very best things.

Heeding that counsel often meant saying no to dinner parties and sporting events on Saturday night so that I could be fresh mentally and physically on Sunday morning. It meant declining certain speaking dates to which I really wanted to say yes.

Sometimes I find such choices hard to make, simply because I like people to approve of me. When a person learns to say no to good things, he runs the risk of making enemies and gaining critics; and who needs more of those? So I find it hard to say no.

I have discovered that most people whose lives are leadership centred face the same challenge. But my father's counsel is foolproof: If we are to command our time, we will have to bite the bullet and say a firm but courteous no to opportunities that are merely good but not best.

Once again that demands, as it did in the ministry of our Lord, a sense of our mission. What are we called to do? What do we do best with our time? What are the necessities without which we cannot get along? Everything else has to be considered negotiable, discretionary, not necessary.

I am drawn to the words C. S. Lewis wrote in *Letters to an American Lady* about the importance of these choices:

> Don't be too easily convinced that God really wants you to do all sorts of work you needn't do. Each must do his duty "in that state of life to which God has called him." Remember that a belief in the virtues of doing for doing's sake is characteristically feminine, characteristically American, and characteristically modern: so that *three* veils may divide you from the correct view! There can be intemperance in work just as in drink. What feels like zeal may be only fidgets or even the flattering of one's self importance . . . By doing what "one's station and its duties" does not demand, one can make oneself less fit for the duties it *does* demand and so commit some injustice. Just you give Mary a little chance as well as Martha.[3]

3. *I Manage Time and Command It Best When I Budget It Far in Advance.* This last principle is the most important; here is where the battle is won or lost.

I have learned the hard way that the principal elements of my time budget have to be in the calendar eight weeks in advance of the date. Eight weeks!

If this is August, then I am already beginning to think through October. And what goes into the calendar? Those non-negotiable aspects of my private world: my spiritual disciplines, my mental disciplines, my Sabbath rest, and of course my commitments to family and special friendships. Then a second tier of priorities will enter the calendar: the schedule of the main work to which I am committed – sermon study, writing, leadership development, and discipling.

As much as possible, all of this is placed in the calendar many, many weeks in advance of the target week, because as I get closer to that week I discover that people move in to make demands upon the available time. Some of them will have legitimate demands, and it is to be hoped there will be space for them.

But others will make demands that are not appropriate. They will inquire about an evening that I have scheduled for the family. Or they will want an hour in a morning reserved for study. How much better my private world is when I allow these activities to *flow around* the priorities and into available slots than when things are the other way around.

It occurred to me one day that my most important time allocations had something in common. They never screamed out immediately when ignored. I could neglect my spiritual disciplines, for example, and God did not seem to shout loudly about it. I could make it just fine for a while. And when I did not allocate time for the family, Gail and the children were generally understanding and forgiving – often more so than certain church members who demanded instant response and attention. And when I set study aside as a priority, I could get away with it for a while. These things could be ignored for a while without adverse consequences. And that is why they were so often crowded out when I did not budget for them in advance. Other less important issues had a way of wedging them aside week after week. Tragically, if they are neglected too long, when family, rest, and spiritual disciplines are finally noticed it is often too late for adverse consequences to be avoided.

When our son, Mark, was in high school, he was a successful athlete; our teenage daughter, Kristen, was an actress and musician. Both were in games and performances. It would have been easy to have missed those events had I not pencilled the dates into the calendar weeks and weeks in advance. My secretary always kept the game schedules in the office calendar, for example, and knew full well not to expect me to commit to anything that would violate those times.

When someone would ask me to meet with him on the afternoon of a game, I was liable to take out my calendar and stroke my chin thoughtfully saying, "I'm sorry, I'm unable to do it that day; I already have a commitment. How about this as an alternative?" I rarely had a problem. The key was in planning and budgeting, weeks in advance.

One needs to ask, what are my non-negotiables? I have discovered that most of us who complain that we are disorganized simply do not know the answer to this question. As a result, the important functions that will make the supreme difference in our effectiveness miss getting into the calendar until it is too late. The consequence? Disorganization and frustration; the non-essentials crowd into the date book before the necessities do. And that is painful over the long run.

The other day a man caught up with me and asked if we could have an early morning breakfast on a certain day. "How early?" I asked.

"You're an early riser," he said. "Why not six?" I looked at my calendar and said, "I'm sorry, I've already got a commitment for that hour; how about seven?" He agreed on seven rather quickly but looked quite surprised that my calendar might reflect plans for that early in the morning.

I did have a commitment for six that morning. In fact it started earlier than that. It was a commitment to God. He was first on the calendar that day where He belongs every day. And it is not the sort of commitment one compromises. Not if one wants to seize time and keep it under control. It is the start of an organized day, an organized life, and an organized private world.

Sector Three

MEMO TO THE DISORGANIZED

If my private world is in order, it will be because I have determined that every day will be for me a day of growth in knowledge and wisdom.

EIGHT

The Better Man Lost

THE ONLY GOLD MEDALS AND BLUE RIBBONS I WON IN my younger years were gained on track and cross-country fields. Although I might have been a more successful runner if I had been tougher on myself, those years of competitive running in prep school and college were nevertheless an opportunity for rich learning experiences in terms of the development of self-discipline and character.

Among all those youthful experiences, the most memorable lesson came at the Penn Relays in Philadelphia one spring day. On that occasion, I was the lead-off man for our prep-school mile relay team, a strategically important position. My objective was to gain the lead in the race and, when I had completed my quarter – mile leg, hand that advantage on to the second runner on our team.

For me to finish that leg out of first place would mean that our second man would receive the relay baton while back among a cluster of runners. There one risked a loss of stride in the jostling and shoving that often took place, and it could cost precious tenths of a second. That time could be quite valuable if the race was closely contested in the final lap.

Since our team had drawn the number-two lane, I was curious to see who had received the "pole," or number-one lane position. It turned out to be a runner from Poly Prep with an impressive record as a sprinter in the 100 meters. We had competed against each other on a couple of other occasions at the shorter distance, and he had beaten me rather badly. Could he do the same when the race was 300 meters longer?

It was obvious that he thought so, because he said as much when we shook hands at the starting line. Looking squarely at me he said, "I'll be waiting for you at the finish line." Today we call that trash talk, a kind of athletic psychological warfare. It partially worked, and for a moment I had to struggle to gain my equilibrium.

The gun went off, and so did the man from Poly Prep. I can remember feeling the sting of the cinders that his spikes shot backward on my shins as he seemed to instantly disappear around the first turn. Meanwhile the remaining seven runners began what looked like a competition for positions number two through eight. Before I had run fifty yards, I began to mentally prepare for finishing in second place, assuming I could make even that happen.

And that is indeed what would have happened – if the race had been shorter. Somewhere around the 300-meter point, however, affairs abruptly changed. The man from Poly Prep, far out in front, suddenly slowed down from sprint to jog. A second later, as I charged around him now running at my peak stride, I could hear him struggling to breathe. He was barely moving. As athletes put it, he was out of gas. I don't remember in what place he finished, but I do know that I was waiting for him at the finish line, trying hard not to gloat.

I learned a valuable lesson that day at the expense of the man from Poly Prep. Inadvertently, he had taught me that even men and women of great talent and energy have to run the *complete* course before they can claim the victory. To be in front at the first turn is meaningless without the endurance to finish strongly. The race must be run at a steady pace all the way to the finish. And a good runner is even prepared to complete the course with a "kick," an extra burst of speed. Athletic talent is of little consequence unless it is matched to adequate endurance.

THE COST OF MENTAL FLABBINESS

I tell this story because it speaks to another segment of our private lives that must be consistent in the process of personal organization. The ordering of our private world cannot take place without strong mental endurance and the intellectual growth this endurance produces.

In our pressurized society, people who are out of shape mentally usually fall victim to ideas and systems that are destructive to the human spirit and to human relationships. They are victimized because they have not taught themselves how to think; nor have they set themselves to the lifelong pursuit of the growth of the mind. Not having the facility of a strong mind, they grow dependent upon the thoughts and opinions of others. Rather than deal with ideas and issues, they reduce themselves to lives full of rules, regulations, and programs.

V. W. Burroughs wrote: "One of the saddest experiences is to awaken at old age and discover that one has been using only a small part of self." He says it quite succinctly. Many of us are always in danger of squandering that enormous wealth of thinking power that God built into humanity at creation. He ordained that we should be *mindful,* not *mindless* people. But mindfulness is a matter of discipline and hard work. Mindlessness is the result of laziness and fear.

The 1978 mass suicide in Guyana by members of the Peoples' Temple is a poignant example of where mindlessness can lead. Allowing Jim Jones to do their thinking for them, the membership courted disaster. They switched off their minds and depended upon the functioning of his. And when Jones's mind ceased working correctly, everyone suffered the consequences. A leader had promised people guidance in the midst of a hostile and angry world. He had offered answers and sustenance. And people signed away their right to independent judgement as the price of such security.

People whose minds are not strengthened for endurance are by no means always unintelligent. They simply have never stopped to think that the use of the mind for the purpose of growth is a necessary part of a God-pleasing lifestyle. It is easy to fall into the trap of allowing the mind to grow flaccid, especially when there are many dominant people all around who would just as soon do our thinking for us.

Such mindlessness can be seen in an unbalanced – and ungodly – family, where one person intimidates all other family members into letting him or her do all the decision-making and opinion-forming. We have many examples of churches where lay people delegate the thinking to a highly dominant pastor. The epistle of 3 John speaks against a man named Diotrephes, a lay leader who, like Jim Jones, had virtually everyone under his control. The Christians simply surrendered their thinking to him.

THE DANGER OF BEING A FAST STARTER

As in a race where the naturally talented runner springs from the starting blocks with a blinding burst of speed, there are those who enjoy fast starts in adult life – not because they are great thinkers or mental giants, but rather because of natural abilities and useful connections. They may have had the benefit of growing up in talented families, where the people around them were highly communicative and gifted in dealing with ideas and problem-solving. As a result, they may have acquired considerable self-confidence at an early age.

Such early exposures teach the young person how to lead, how to compete against others, and how to handle himself in difficult situations. The result could be called "premature success." And premature success is often more an obstacle than a help.

The premature succeeder is usually a fast learner, able to acquire expertise with minimum effort. He is usually blessed with good health and abundant energy. He can talk his way into or out of anything, it seems. And he may conclude that he can do just about anything he sets his mind to, because things appear to come easily to him.

How long things can go on this way is anyone's guess. For a lifetime, I suppose, in certain cases. But my observation is that somewhere in his early thirties, indications of possible trouble will begin to show in the life of the naturally talented fast starter. There may be the first hints that the rest of the race in life will have to be run on endurance and discipline and not talent. And like the runner from Poly Prep, he may start to see that the slower but better-conditioned runners are beginning to catch up.

In my counselling I have met many people who are struggling through midlife for this reason. I see a startling number of exhausted, mentally empty people who have stopped growing and are spending their lives in the pursuit of little more than amusement.

I use the word amusement because of its literal meaning. It suggests function without thought (a meaning "without"; muse, "to think"). Functioning without thought leads to a feeling of personal disorganization. Who are the people who function without thought? They can easily be folk of whom it was said twenty years before, "He is going places; he can't miss." It can be the preacher who at the age of twenty-one had unusual pulpit powers, the salesman who began his career with a remarkable record of completed deals, the woman who graduated valedictorian of her class. It tends to be those who never realized that the mind must be pushed, filled, stretched, and forced in order to function. Natural talent takes such people only so far and lets them down long before the race is finished.

THE LIFE OF THE MIND

The mind must be *trained* to think, to analyze, to innovate. People fully organized in their private worlds *work* at being thinkers. Their minds are alert and alive, taking on fresh amounts of information every day, regularly producing new discoveries and conclusions. They commit themselves to the daily exercise of the mind.

"I possessed information without knowledge, opinions without principles, instincts without beliefs," writes David Denby as he takes a hard look at himself.[1] That's a scary discovery; it is a call to re-evaluate one's way of looking at things. It's what Paul was thinking about when he wrote: "Do not be conformed to the pattern of this world, but be transformed by the renewing of your mind" (Romans 12:2).

Paul saw our alternatives very clearly. The person who does not know how to think will be relentlessly shaped and influenced by the dominant culture around him or her. But the transformed person (presumably transformed by the Spirit of Christ) will be busy thinking, reflecting, and making independent conclusions about the meaning of life and reality.

You see this throughout the scriptural stories of great men and women. Esther, who ascended to the position of Persian queen under strange circumstances, was chided by her mentor, Mordecai, when he became aware of a growing plot to wipe out the Jews. When Esther initially resisted his encouragement to confront the king on this matter, he wrote, "Do not think that because you are in the king's house you alone of all the Jews will escape. For if you remain silent at this time, relief and deliverance for the Jews will arise from another place, but you and your father's family will perish. And who knows but that you have come to royal position for such a time as this?" (Est. 4:13-14).

Think, Esther, think! That's Mordecai's message. But what if one has never been trained to think?

"No vital Christianity is possible unless at least three aspects of it are developed," wrote Elton Trueblood. "These three are the inner life of devotion, the outer life of service, and the *intellectual life of rationality* [italics added]."[2] The third aspect is the easiest for many evangelicals to ignore, thinking it too worldly (as some like to say) and offensive to the gospel. But the dulling of the mind leads to ultimate disorganization of the private world.

I understand premature success because I too discovered in my early thirties that I was coasting on natural talent and not giving adequate attention to the development of my mind. I began to see that unless I did something about it, my mind would not adequately serve me in later years when I wanted to be running at peak mental stride, doing and giving my very best.

For me it meant that if I was going to become a more effective preacher, a more sensitive understander of hurting people, and a more useful leader, I would have to take seriously the challenge of sharpening my mental capacities so I could deal with my public world. Although I was not entirely asleep intellectually, I was not doing the hard, disciplined work that would help me to be the innovative and seminal person I thought God wanted me to be.

No wonder I felt the pangs of disorganization when I faced situations in which I was not smart enough to understand what was going on. Like someone with a weight too heavy to lift, I found myself more and more trying to hoist ideas and perplexities that I was not mentally strong enough to get off the ground.

"The man of action has the present," wrote Oliver Wendell Holmes, "but the thinker commands the future from his study."

Although evangelical Christians have made an outspoken commitment to Christian education, there has not always been a high enough value placed upon the development of the mind. Few of us have fully appreciated the contrast between gatherers of details and rules and skilled handlers of truth. There may be some who know a little about a lot of things, but that does not guarantee that many of us know how to think deeply and insightfully about what we know.

I have watched men and women who have pressed enormous amounts of information about the Bible into their heads. They have learned to speak a rich vocabulary of correct Christian jargon. Their prayers can be so smooth-sounding that all those about them sit in awe. We think them to be spiritual people. But at other times, we begin to see that they are rigid and inflexible, impervious to change and innovation. Their response to any serious challenge to their thought is a burst of anger or accusation.

Like others, I am convinced that Christians ought to be the strongest, broadest, most creative thinkers in the world. Again, it was Paul who said that as Christians we are given the mind of Christ. This provides a potential intellectual breadth that the unregenerate mind does not possess. It offers an eternal, timeless perspective in which to think. In Christ there is a foundation of truth that ought to make our ideas, our analysis of things, and our innovations among the most powerful of the age. But because there is an essential laziness and internal disorganization in many Christian lives, this is not always the case. We are forfeiting one of the great gifts God provided through Christ.

Missionary evangelist Stanley Jones wrote:

> Swami Shivananda, a famous swami in India, used to tell his disciples: "Kill the mind and then, and then only, can you meditate." The Christian position is "Thou shalt love the Lord thy God with all thy mind {► the intellectual nature}, with all thy heart {► the emotional nature}, with all thy soul {► the willing nature} and with all thy strength {► the physical nature}". The total person is to love him – mind, emotion, will, strength. But the "strength" might mean the strength of all three. Some love him with the strength of the mind and the weakness of the emotion – the intellectualist in religion; some love him with the strength of emotion and the weakness of the mind – the sentimentalist in religion; some love him with the strength of the will and the weakness of emotion – the man of iron who is not very approachable. *But loving God with the strength of the mind, the strength of the emotion, and the strength of the will – that makes the truly Christian and the truly balanced and the truly strong character.* [italics added][3]

For many years Admiral Hyman Rickover was the head of the United States Nuclear Navy. His admirers and his critics held strongly opposing views about the stern and demanding admiral. For many years every officer aboard a nuclear submarine was personally interviewed

THE BETTER MAN LOST

and approved by Rickover. Those who went through those interviews usually came out shaking in fear, anger, or total intimidation. Among them was ex-President Jimmy Carter, who, years ago, applied for service under Rickover. This is his account of a Rickover interview:

> I had applied for the nuclear submarine program, and Admiral Rickover was interviewing me for the job. It was the first time I met Admiral Rickover, and we sat in a large room by ourselves for more than two hours, and he let me choose any subjects I wished to discuss. Very carefully, I chose those about which I knew most at the time – current events, seamanship, music, literature, naval tactics, electronics, gunnery – and he began to ask me a series of questions of increasing difficulty. In each instance, he soon proved that I knew relatively little about the subject I had chosen.

> He always looked right into my eyes, and he never smiled. I was saturated with cold sweat.

> Finally, he asked a question and I thought I could redeem myself. He said, "How did you stand in your class at the Naval Academy?" Since I had completed my sophomore year at Georgia Tech before entering Annapolis as a plebe, I had done very well, and I swelled my chest with pride and answered, "Sir, I stood fifty-ninth in a class of 820!" I sat back to wait for the congratulations – which never came. Instead, the question: "Did you do your best?" I started to say, "Yes, sir," but I remembered who this was and recalled several of the many times at the Academy when I could have learned more about our allies, our enemies, weapons, strategy, and so forth. I was just human. I finally gulped and said, "No, sir, I didn't always do my best."

> He looked at me for a long time, and then turned his chair around to end the interview. He asked one final question, which I have never been able to forget – or

to answer. He said, "Why not?" I sat there for a while, shaken, and then slowly left the room.[4]

That encounter became the thought-starter for Carter's book *Why Not the Best?* And it is a worthwhile story to ponder. Does not the man or woman who claims to walk with Christ owe the Creator excellence in terms of thought?

Thinking is the amazing capacity God has given the human being to discover and observe the stuff of creation, to compare and contrast each of its parts, and when possible, to use them properly so as to reflect the glory of the Creator. Thinkers see old things in new ways; they analyze hypotheses, separating out the true from the false. Thinkers sometimes describe old truths in new words and forms; they help others to see how applications to life can be made. Thinkers make bold decisions, help us see new visions, and overcome obstacles in previously unseen ways.

These are not merely the exercises of the great and the brilliant. They are the tasks of everyone with a healthy mind. As with physical bodies, some of us may be stronger than others, but that does not relieve us of the responsibility of using our bodies or our minds.

It is said that even though he held over a thousand patents, Thomas Edison felt he could only claim one invention – the phonograph – as his original idea. All his other "inventions," he said, were adaptations and improvements upon ideas that other people had left undeveloped.

It would do us good to see ourselves as sponges. Throughout the expanse of creation God has hidden things for humankind to discover, to enjoy, and with which to perceive the nature of the Creator Himself. We should sponge it all up. Proverbs 25:2 says, "It is the glory of God to conceal a matter, but the glory of kings is to search out a matter."

The work of the first man and woman was to discover and identify things God had made. Because of their disobedience against God's laws, some of the opportunity for that kind of marvellous work was forfeited. They now had to worry more about surviving in a hostile world than continuing to discover what was in it. The nature of work abruptly changed. I have a conviction that the heavenly life will in some way recover that original form of work.

But the principle and privilege of discovery still prevails in part. Some discoveries come through hard physical labour, such as digging gold out of the side of a hill. Other discoveries are made as we observe the progress of living things in the plant, animal, and human kingdoms. And much of the exploration of creation is done purely within the mind. We dig, as it were, and uncover ideas and truths; then we turn around to express them artistically, worshipfully, and inventively.

Thinking is a great work. It is best done with a mind that has trained and is in shape just as competitive running is done with a body that has trained and is in shape. The best kind of thinking is accomplished when it is done in the context of reverence for God's kingly reign over all creation. It is sad to see great thinking and artistic work accomplished by men and women who have no interest in uncovering knowledge of the Creator. They think and innovate purely for self-aggrandizement or for the development of a human system that assumes it can get along without God.

Some Christians appear to be afraid to think. They mistake the gathering of facts, doctrinal systems, and lists of rules for thinking. They are uneasy when dealing with ambiguity. And they do not see the significance of wrestling with great ideas if they cannot always come up with easily packaged answers. The consequences are a drift toward mediocrity in personal living and mental activity and a loss of much that God meant for His children to enjoy as they walk through creation discovering His handiwork. Life under such circumstances becomes *amusement,* function without thought.

The unthinking Christian does not realize it, but he is dangerously absorbed into the culture about him. Because his mind is untrained and unfilled, it lacks the ability to produce the hard questions with which the world needs to be challenged. The challenge for the modern Christian in a secular society may be to ask prophetic questions before there is going to be an opportunity to provide Christ-oriented answers.

Sometimes, because of the massive amounts of information bombarding us regularly, the unthinking Christian longs to run in retreat, leaving heavy thinking up to a few elite Christian leaders or theologians.

Harry Blamires, in an insightful book called *The Christian Mind,* asks where there are Christians with minds sharp enough to confront a culture that steadily drifts away from God. He calls for people who think "Christianly" about great moral issues. His fear, which I share, is that we fool ourselves into thinking that we are thinking people when we are not. With a stinging rebuke against the Christian public, he wrote:

> Christianity is emasculated of its intellectual relevance. It remains a vehicle of spirituality and moral guidance at the individual level perhaps; at the communal level it is little more than an expression of sentimentalized togetherness.[5]

When the Christian's mind becomes dull, he can fall prey to the propaganda of a non-Christian scheme of things, led by people who have not neglected their thinking powers – and have simply outthought us.

Just as my coach once taught me to train my body in order to finish the entire race, so I had to learn what others are having to learn: that the mind also has to be trained. The private world of the Christian will be weak, defenceless, and disorganized if serious attention has not been given to this sector of intellectual growth.

The man from Poly Prep was a better runner, but he lost. He lost because 100 yards of talent is not good enough for 440 yards of race.

When I once evaluated the order of the intellectual sector of my private world, I thankfully came to see that a few natural gifts or a few years of education were never going to make me the man God wanted to use in any part of the world where He wanted me to do work. If I was going to endure and become useful to the level of my potential, it would not be because I had talents or degrees, but because I had learned to take the muscles of my mind and work them into shape.

I had to become a thinker. I had to become conversant with the directions that history was taking. I needed to know how to grapple with the great ideas of humankind. And I had to learn how to make independent judgements about what I was seeing. It was time for me to start working – hard. Other runners were catching up, and the race was far from over. I didn't want to be a better man in the first turn and a loser at the finish line because I had talent but no endurance.

In his journal, Oswald Chambers wrote:

> A great fear has been at work in my mind and God has used it to arouse me to prayer. I came across a man whom I knew years ago, a mighty man of God, and now ten years have gone and I meet him again – garrulous and unenlivened [shallow and superficial]. How many men seem to become like that after forty years of age! The fear of sloth and indulgence has come home with a huge fear and fairly driven me to God to keep me from ever forgetting what I owe him.[6]

Apparently, Chambers was greatly marked by this encounter of which he wrote, because he reflected upon it again sometime later: "I hate to meet a man whom I have met ten years ago and find that he is at precisely the same point, neither moderated nor quickened nor experienced but simply stiffened."

Think about it!

MEMO TO THE DISORGANIZED

If my private world is in order, it will be because I seek to use all I learn in service to others, as Christ did.

NINE

The Sadness of a Book Never Read

MY WIFE, GAIL, AND I WERE BROWSING IN AN OLD bookstore one day looking for those special titles among second-hand books that are such a delight when found. Gail found a copy of a biography of Daniel Webster that had been published in the 1840s. It looked interesting, and since we are lovers of biographies, she purchased the book.

The cover of the book appeared worn enough to convey the notion that it had been well read. One could imagine that it had been a prized edition in the library of several generations of a New England family. Perhaps it had been loaned out on a number of occasions and brought enlightenment to a dozen different readers.

Not so! When Gail began to leaf through the old book, she discovered that the printer had failed to properly cut the pages, and many of them could not be opened until one took a blade and cut them apart. The uncut pages were clear evidence that the book had never been read! It looked on the outside as if it had been constantly used. But if it had, it was only in gracing a library shelf, or playing doorstop, or providing height to a small child so that he could sit and reach the table while he ate. The book may have been used, but it certainly had never been read.

The Christian who is not growing intellectually is like a book whose many pages remain unopened and unread. Like the book, he may be of some value, but not nearly as much as if he had chosen to sharpen and develop his mind.

As a body grows flabby when it is not exposed to physical labour or challenging exercise, so the mind weakens, gets out of shape, when it is not given proper training. I'd never really given much thought to thinking as a discipline until I read an old book (1928) by a French writer, Ernest Dimnet, called *The Art of Thinking*. I love these lines of his. When you read them, remember . . . they are almost seventy-five years old.

> Enter Thinker. We have all seen him standing amidst the surprised, incredulous and often silly group of non-thinkers. Sometimes he is a very simple man, the roadside mechanic slowly walking out of his garage. Round the car two or three men, hot with ineffective guessing, are still talking excitedly when the taciturn man appears; for an hour they have talked, tried and failed. They stop and not another word is heard. The intelligent eyes of the artisan, helped by his seeming infallible hands, go over the organs of the machine; meanwhile we know that his mind is going over dozens of hypotheses which to us are only riddles. Soon the trouble is found. Sometimes the man smiles. At what? At whom? I often wonder. At any rate we have felt the presence of a brain.

Dimnet has other examples, but I love this one best of all. How clever! A mechanic as a thinker. I would never have thought of it as an example. But it is wonderful. And I can picture all the other "know-it-alls" standing around, quiet in their incredulity. "We have felt the presence of a brain, " he said. No harm reading a masterful sentence twice.

"The thinker," Dimnet later wrote,

. . . is pre-eminently a [person] who sees where others do not. The novelty of what he says, its character as a sort of revelation, the charm that attaches to it, all come from the fact that he sees. He seems to be head and shoulders above the crowd, or to be walking on the ridgeway while others trudge at the bottom. Independence is the word which describes the moral aspect of this capacity for vision.[1]

In his best days, this was what Solomon must have been. A man who looked into things seeking meaning. One who could put ideas together and come up with sensible conclusions. One who loved the stuff of creation and wasn't afraid to search out the knowledge of it.

[Solomon] spoke three thousand proverbs and his songs numbered a thousand and five. He described plant life, from the cedar of Lebanon to the hyssop that grows out of walls. He also taught about animals and birds, reptiles and fish. Men of all nations came to listen to Solomon's wisdom. (1 Kings 4:32-34)

How do we encourage the development of people like this? People of substance who speak thoughtfully. Who do not capitulate to shallow ideas. Who are not intellectually lazy, living under the dominance of other, more strident minds. Who are able to search the nooks and crannies of possibilities and summon deep judgement. Who are not captive to ideologies that leave no room for independent conclusions or actions.

PUTTING YOURSELF IN A GROWTH MODE

When a person sets out to deliberately use his mind for the purpose of growth and development as a person, new order comes into his private world. His mind – an organ largely undeveloped in many people – comes alive with new possibility when he sets himself in what I call a growth mode.

There are at least three objectives in developing the intellectual dimension of our private worlds. Let me offer them to you as a scheme for mental development.

1. The Mind Must Be Disciplined to Think Christianly. I understand this objective because I grew up in a Christian context and had the full advantage of Christian teaching from infancy.

To think Christianly means to look at our world from the perspective that it is made and owned by God, that what we do with creation will have to be accounted for, and that it is important to make choices according to the laws of God. The Bible calls this stewardship. Christian thinking looks at all issues and ideas from the standpoint of what God desires and what might give honour to Him.

A person who has not enjoyed the advantage of a lifelong Christian context is not liable to gain that total perspective easily. If he becomes a follower of Christ at a later age, it will be particularly bothersome to compare his instincts and reactions to those of more mature believers. He will tend to be hard on himself, wondering if he will ever get ahead in matters of faith.

For this kind of person, thinking will be done more by *commitment* than by Christian instinct. In other words, the newer Christian's reaction to a problem or opportunity is apt to be a non-Christian one, and he will then have to reverse and replace it with a learned Christian response.

The person who thinks Christianly by background probably thinks with all the proper reactions, unless he deliberately chooses to embrace a life of rebellion. But – and this is important – whether or not he will follow up the Christian mental response with Christian action is another matter. The mental response without the action is of little use.

I describe these two styles of thought because I have found it to be helpful to people, especially younger Christians who are struggling with the meaning of spiritual growth. They wonder why they are always just a second behind the older Christians and seem unable to catch up. The key is often in Christian acculturation, which is certainly an advantage and testifies to the importance of the Christian family. This kind of Christian acculturation is becoming less and less frequent as the world around us grows increasingly secular and drifts from a Christian base.

For the new Christian, mental growth will be in part the cultivation of the Christian perspective, the Christian response to life, and the Christian value system in the marketplace.

The long-term Christian has a struggle of a different sort. Although he may have an instinctive Christian reaction to most situations, his commitment may not be as enthusiastic as the newly converted believer. He simply assumes that Christianized mechanisms will work automatically. And this can be very dangerous over a period of time. Thinking Christianly without a regular renewal of our commitment to Christ leads to a deadness of religion, a boring faith, an ineffective witness to God. And we who have grown up with the gospel of Christ have to be very careful to avoid this.

2. *The Mind Must Be Taught to Observe and Appreciate the Messages God Has Written in Creation.* "The heavens are telling of the glory of God" (Ps. 19:1). Everything God made – even human beings – has as its key purpose the reflection of the honour of God.

Unfortunately, the power of sin has tarnished the capacity of some aspects of creation to reflect that hon. In fact, sin first appears to have done its job on humanity; then, through men and women, sin systematically trashed everything else in creation. But where man has not been able to confuse the issue, the creation continues to shout out its message: God the Creator be praised!

The growing mind, filled with the love of Christ, searches creation for these messages. Because of our spiritual and natural gifts, each of us is able to see and hear them in particular areas more than in others. And we are enabled to take this creation material and identify it, shape it, reconfigure it, or in other ways use it so that God is further glorified. The carpenter works with wood; the physician listens to the body; the musician arranges sounds; the executive manages people; the educator trains students; the researcher analyzes, innovates, and implements with the elements of the universe.

We develop our minds for these tasks and rejoice as we do them for all that God is revealing to us out of His loving heart.

3. *The Mind Must Be Trained to Pursue Information, Ideas, and Insights for the Purpose of Serving the People of the Public World.* The development of the mind makes it possible for men and women to be servants to the generation in which they live. I think of the contributions of missionary physician Paul Brand, who is credited with the development of surgical procedures that have restored the use of limbs to those suffering from Hansen's disease (leprosy). We have all been enriched by the mind of C. S. Lewis in literature or John Perkins in the area of race relations. And there are men and women whose names are not as well known: a young civil engineer who uses his expertise to help build a hydroelectric dam in Ecuador; an accountant who gives precious time to help disadvantaged people restructure themselves financially; a builder who goes into the inner city and teaches men and women to rehabilitate and winterize old houses; and a computer operator who

gives time to teach immigrant children to read. All of these are using their minds in ministry to others.

We do not develop our intellects merely for our own personal advancement, but we put our thinking power to work for the use of others. I remember this when I push myself in my reading and filing: I am collecting the raw material that will become a sermon or book of encouragement or insight for others one day. As my mind grows, it may make possible the growth of others.

ORGANIZING THE MIND TO MAKE IT GROW

Looking back across the early years of my life, I recall once coming to the startling realization that although I had amassed enormous amounts of information about many things, I had never really pushed myself to be an aggressive thinker. In fact, I am not sure I had ever learned to love learning.

My father was a strong and dominating thinker. It was as if he did the family's thinking for us. To express a thought contrary to his when I was a boy was no simple matter, and I often lost the courage to do so. My problem! So when I "graduated" from my family of origin, I had some catching up to do in the area of original thinking. And I often wonder if I have ever caught up.

Moving through my educational years, I tended to be one of those who played the margins. "Tell me what it takes to pass this course," I said, "and I'll give it to you." With rare exceptions, I adopted that philosophy throughout high school, college, and graduate school. Occasionally I would be confronted by an instructor who saw through that limited view and would push me toward a higher excellence. I never stopped to ask myself why I appreciated those instructors more than the others. It was indeed fun to be stretched, to have something better than the average pulled out of me.

But when I finally left the formal education process behind, there was no one to push or pull me, no one to require intellectual excellence except myself. And soon I learned that I would have to accept full responsibility for my own mental growth. That was when I achieved intellectual puberty. For the first time I became serious about learning how to think and learn on my own.

How does one go about this process of intellectual organization in the private world? Let me suggest several ways:

- ## We Grow by Becoming Listeners

My intellectual organization began when I learned to listen. For someone like me who enjoys talking, listening can be a challenge. But if a person is not a listener, he denies his mind a major source of information by which to grow.

Perhaps the first step in becoming a listener is to learn to ask questions. I have rarely met a person or been in a situation where there was not something valuable worth learning. On many occasions, I have had to generate listening by first asking questions. That has meant learning how to be good at asking questions. Right questions elicit valuable information for the purposes of growth. I like to ask men and women about their jobs, where they met their spouses, what they have been reading about, what they consider their greatest present challenges, and where they find God most alive in their lives. The answers are always useful.

In the process of becoming a listener, I have come to see that most people are eager to share something of themselves. Many older people rarely have anyone to listen to them, and they are usually wellsprings of insight. Suffering people, people under stress and tension, have much to share with those who can learn to ask the right questions. And in asking we not only learn, but we are also able to encourage and love.

We particularly need to learn to listen to older people and children. They all have stories to tell that enrich the mind and the heart. Children simplify things, often with brutal honesty. Older people bring the perspective of their long years on issues. Suffering people also help us understand what are the truly important matters of life. There is something to learn from all people if we are only willing to sit at their feet and humble ourselves enough to ask the right questions.

A second part of mental growth by listening came when I started to visit people at their places of labour to see what they do, meet the people with whom they work, and so learn something of the particular challenges they face. I pushed myself to gain a new appreciation of the differing sorts of contributions people around me are making to my world. I enjoy asking men and women about their vocations: "Tell me what it takes to do a job like yours with excellence. What are the great challenges a person faces? Where do you confront ethical and moral questions? What is there about this sort of task that brings on fatigue or discouragement? Do you ever ask yourself about the ways God is present in this job?"

A third way of growing through listening comes when we listen to mentors. Throughout my life God has surrounded me with a chain of men and women who believed in me, cared for me, and tried to make a contribution to the bringing forth of whatever potential God had placed in me. I am grateful that I was taught by my parents to listen to such people, for many of my colleagues tended to slough off the counsel and wisdom of such mentors and so lost valuable information.

Fourth, I can suggest that growth always comes when we also listen to our critics. And that is not an easy thing for any of us to do. Dawson Trotman, the founder of the Navigators, had a good method for handling all criticisms directed at himself. No matter how unfair the criticism might seem to be, he would always take it into his prayer closet and in effect spread it before the Lord. Then he would say, "Lord, please show me the kernel of truth hidden in this criticism."

The truth may certainly be small on occasion, but it is always worth finding and thinking through. I have been grateful to learn of Dawson Trotman's secret. It has saved me countless bad moments when I might have otherwise been tempted to be defensive when criticized. Instead I began to learn to grow at the hands of my critics. I have seldom ever heard a criticism about myself that didn't indeed contain a kernel of useful truth. Some of the kernels have been on the small side, but they were there.

When I mentally list the most important truths on which I have based my own character and personality development, I am astonished to discover that a large majority of them came through painful situations where someone, either out of love or anger, rebuked or criticized me soundly. I carry with me the memory of a time when my missiology professor at Denver Seminary, Dr. Raymond Buker, approached me at the end of a special convocation where I had read a paper on some moral issue that was burning in the hearts of the student generation of that day. I had cut two of his classes that day to prepare the paper, and it had not gone unnoticed.

"Gordon," he said, "the paper you read tonight was a good one, but it wasn't a great one. Would you like to know why?"

I wasn't sure I really wanted to know because I anticipated a bit of humiliation coming my way, but I swallowed hard and told Dr. Buker that I would like to hear his analysis.

"The paper wasn't a great one," he said as he thumped his finger on my chest, "because you sacrificed the routine to write it."

In pain I learned one of the most important lessons I ever needed to learn. Because my time as a Christian leader has been generally my own to use as I please, it would be very easy to avoid routine, unspectacular duties, and give myself only to the exciting things that come along. But most of life is lived in the routine, and Buker was right: The man or woman who learns to make peace with routine responsibilities and obligations will make the greatest contributions in the long run.

But I would not have learned that lesson and grown from it, at least at that point in my life, if there had not been a man willing to rebuke me and if I had not been willing to listen and learn.

We grow through listening, aggressive listening: asking questions, watching intently what is happening around us, taking note of the good or ill consequences that befall people as a result of their choice making.

• **We Grow Through Reading**

A second way we grow is through reading. In our age of mass media, the younger generation is finding it harder and harder to acquire the discipline of reading, and that may be one of the greatest losses of our time. Nothing substitutes for what can be found when we embrace the world of books.

Paul gave evidence of his own hunger for reading when he wrote to Timothy asking for parchments and books. Even at that older age, he was anxious to grow. Some of us are not naturally given to reading, and it is hard for us. But to whatever extent we can press ourselves in this direction, we should acquire the habit of reading systematically.

My wife and I are students of biography, and there is hardly a time in our home when the two of us are not making our way through two or three biographical accounts. These books have poured priceless insights into our minds.

Others will be drawn to psychology, theology, history, or good fiction. But all of us need to have at least one good book going at all times, more if possible. When I visit with pastors who are struggling with their own effectiveness, I often ask, "What are you reading lately?" It is almost predictable that if a pastor is struggling with failure in his ministry, he will be unable to name a title or an author that he has been reading in recent days. If he is not reading, the chances are strong that he is not growing. And if he is not growing, then he may rapidly slip into ineffectiveness.

It has been a long time since America struggled through the hostage crisis in Iran. Those of us who remember that ordeal will not forget one woman who seemed to stand out from the other fifty or more victims that were held for more than four hundred days. Katherine Koob became an inspiration to many in the embassy and here in the United States. When she returned to her home and was able to describe what kept her both sane and strong while in such conditions, she readily acknowledged that it was the reading and memorizing she had done throughout her life. In her mind was stored an almost infinite amount of material from which she drew strength and resolve as well as the truth with which to comfort others.

In my own disciplines, I have tried to set aside a minimum of an hour each day for the purpose of reading. I have found that one should never read without a pencil in hand to mark salient passages, and I have developed a simple series of codes that will remind me of impressive thoughts or quotes worth clipping and filing for future use.

As I read, I jot down key thoughts and ideas, which become the grist for sermons or articles. Not infrequently an insight jumps out that can be of value to someone I know. It has often been a form of ministry to make a copy of that particular quote or reference and send it along as a piece of encouragement or instruction.

If an author has been particularly stimulating to my mind and heart, I will attempt to acquire everything he or she has written. And I will take careful note of bibliographies, footnotes, and indexes for material worth checking into myself.

Over the years, I have learned to ask anyone I know to be a student or reader of any kind, "What are you reading?" If the person can suggest a half dozen titles, I am most grateful and put them on a reading list. You can always tell the readers in a group when someone mentions a particularly excellent book. The readers are the ones who immediately take out notebook or reference card and jot down the name and author.

• We Grow Through Disciplined Study

A third way to grow mentally is through the discipline of study. The amount of time spent studying will vary for all of us and will have a lot to do with our vocations. Preachers simply have to study if they are going to provide the sort of pulpit "feeding" that they have been mandated to do.

In my earliest years of ministry, when this business of mental growth had not yet become a discipline for me, most of my study was what I now call defensive study. By that I mean that I studied frantically simply because I had an upcoming sermon to preach or talk to give. And all my study was centred on the completion of that task.

But later I discovered the importance of something I now call offensive study. This is study that has as its objective the gathering of large clusters of information and insight out of which future sermons and talks, books, and articles may grow. In the former kind of study, one is restricted to one chosen subject. In the latter, one is exploring, turning up truth and understanding from scores of sources. Both forms of study, offensive and defensive, are necessary in my life.

We grow when we pursue the discipline of offensive study. This is done through reading, taking occasional courses that stretch our minds, taking on challenges that force us to learn new things, and exploring various disciplines for the sheer joy of learning more about God's world.

I found that summer was an ideal time for great offensive study; winter was not. Each year I set aside certain books and projects with which I wished to acquaint myself, and when the summer months provided extra space, I got busy. I hoped that by the end of the summer I would be ready to move into the heavier months of the year with considerable amounts of raw material in my notebooks for sermons and Bible studies throughout the coming church year.

As I mentioned earlier in this book, my own study time has always been best accomplished in the early-morning hours. But in the past I was able to achieve it only because I'd budgeted space for it in the calendar far in advance of the date. When I cheated on the time, I almost always ended up regretting it. Studying was a date in the calendar that should never have been broken.

I have always enjoyed the support of a wife who protected and encouraged my study time, and that was a part of her growth as well. In our early years of marriage and ministry she had to learn the importance of offensive and defensive study just as I had to. As a young wife, when she saw me reading a book or sitting at my desk, she didn't hesitate to interrupt me. After all, it was easy to surmise, what is a thirty-second interruption for a question or a quick break to take out the garbage?

But Gail came to see that study is hard work for me and that interruptions often shatter mental momentum. With that realization, she not only became a protector of my time but a creator of it, skillfully admonishing me if she caught me wasting any of it or procrastinating on my commitments. None of my books would ever have been written if she had not determined with me that my writing was part of the call of God on my life and that I would need her support as well as her prodding.

Some months ago I led a seminar for pastors on the subject of preaching, and discussed the matters of study and preparation. Since a number of spouses were present when I spoke, I said to the group, "Now, some of you may be tempted to think that when your spouse is reading, they are really expending second-class time. So you are liable to feel free to interrupt them on impulse. What you need to realize is that they are working every bit as much as the carpenter who is in his shop sharpening the blade of a saw. Within reason, you ought not only to avoid interrupting your spouses, but also to try your best to maximize their privacy if you want them to grow in effectiveness."

A couple of months later, a couple came to me at another meeting where I was giving some talks. They were hand in hand and both beaming. The young man extended his hand and said, "We've come to thank you for changing our lives."

Since I'm not given to thinking that I can change lives very often, I was curious to know what I had done. The wife responded, "We were present at your seminar on preaching a few months back, and you told us about the importance of reading and studying as work. You emphasized the guarding of one another's times for that. Remember?"

Yes, I certainly remembered.

"I realized," she went on to say, "that I'd never seen my husband's reading and study from that perspective. I promised God that I would do things differently when we got home – "

" – and it's changed my life," the young pastor said. "We're grateful to you."

Studying means developing good filing systems to store my information so that it is never wasted. It means making sacrifices to acquire a good library of reference books. But most of all, it means determination and discipline. And the result is always growth.

One more comment about the importance of studying for all of us. I have talked primarily about pastors because that is my world, and because study is so important to pastors. But I am speaking in principle to all Christians, to all men and women. I have realized the importance not only of my wife's making it possible for me to study but of my making it possible for her to study. This is a mutual discipline to which we encourage one another – both of us should be engaging in growth of the mind.

I want to make clear that this means that we who are husbands need to ask whether or not we are creating and guarding time for our wives to read and study. In the process of marriage counselling, we talk to many couples whose problem is uneven intellectual growth. After ten or fifteen years of marital relationship, one is growing while the other is not. Frankly, we most often encounter the problem of the wife's continuing to maintain intellectual momentum into her forties while the husband prefers sitting in front of the television set. But the problem can work both ways.

You can recognize students of every age primarily because they tend to be note takers. Many years ago Gail and I adopted a special-size notebook paper and bought dozens of loose-leaf binders. All of our notes go into those books under special topical codes. We go virtually nowhere without paper so that we are ready to record the thoughts of someone who might come across our path and have something significant to say. One never knows when he will turn up a book or come upon an experience worth recording for future reference.

The Christian who wants to grow will always take notes when sermons are being preached or Bible classes are being taught. It is one practical way of asserting faith that God is going to give the listener something that will be useful in the future in the service of others. Good note taking is one way to store the information and insights that are constantly coming at us, and therefore to take advantage of all the possible growth that is available to us.

The Old Testament scribe Ezra believed in the growth of the mind. "And Ezra set himself to study the law of the Lord, to do it, and to teach its statutes in all of Israel" (7:10). The order of this description of personal growth in a man's private world is worth noting: He studied; he did what he learned; he shared what was worthwhile. Ezra was a professional student of sorts, putting in far more time than any of us will ever do. But he set a great precedent. And because his mind and spirit were full, God tapped Ezra for the gigantic task of leading a large task force of men across the wilderness to rebuild Jerusalem.

If you were to come to our home today and take that old Webster biography off the shelf, you would discover that we have slit open every page so that we could read the story of that great American's life. The book still looks terribly worn, but now it is worn for the right reason: it has finally been read!

Like the book when we found it, many people show the outer marks of the wear and tear of life. But inside large areas of their private world remain unopened. They are disorganized within because they have never stretched and conditioned their minds to handle the information and challenges of the age. They have not taken advantage of all that God has placed here for us to discover, enjoy, and use.

But when we take seriously the growth and development of our minds, a beautiful thing happens. We come to know God more fully, and we are infinitely more useful in the service of others, for in just the way that creation was originally designed, we – our sharpened minds – begin to reflect the glory of God also.

What a beautiful thing to see: a human being in God's world with a sharpened mind, having opened every page with insight and truth.

Sector Four

THE SADNESS OF A BOOK NEVER READ

MEMO TO THE DISORGANIZED

If my private world is in order, it will be because I regularly choose to enlarge the spiritual centre of my life.

TEN

Order in the Garden

HOWARD RUTLEDGE, A UNITED STATES AIR FORCE PILOT, was shot down over North Vietnam during the early stages of the war. He spent several miserable years in the hands of his captors before being released at the war's conclusion.

In his book *In the Presence of Mine Enemies,* he reflects upon the inner resources (or lack of same) from which he drew in those arduous days when life seemed so intolerable.

> During those longer periods of enforced reflection it became so much easier to separate the important from the trivial, the worthwhile from the waste. For example, in the past, I usually worked or played hard on Sundays and had no time for church. For years Phyllis [his wife] had encouraged me to join the family at church. She never nagged or scolded – she just kept hoping. But I was too busy, too preoccupied, to spend one or two short hours a week thinking about the really important things.

> Now the sights and sounds and smells of death were all around me. My hunger for spiritual food soon outdid my hunger for a steak. Now I wanted to know about that part of me that will never die. Now I wanted to talk about God and Christ and the church. But in Heartbreak [the name POWS gave their prison

camp] solitary confinement, there was no pastor, no Sunday School teacher, no Bible, no hymnbook, no community of believers to guide and sustain me. I had completely neglected the spiritual dimension of my life. *It took prison to show me how empty life is without God.* [italics added][1]

It took the pressure of a POW camp to show Rutledge that there was a centre to his private world that he had been neglecting virtually all of his life. I like to refer to this centre as a person's spirit; others call it the soul. You can't physiologically locate the spiritual centre of a person's private world, but it is there. It is eternal, and it is the point at which we most intimately commune with our heavenly Father. The spirit can never lose its eternal nature, but it can exist in a state of such disorganization that almost no communion with God is possible. That usually leads to a general chaos in other parts of one's private world.

I like Wallace Hamilton's way of describing the natural state of a person's interior life: "Within each of us there is a herd of wild horses all wanting to run loose."

The Christian is theologically convinced of the existence of the soul. But many Christians struggle with the quality of life within that centre. At least that is the impression I get when I listen for very long to those who are willing to talk about the meaning of private spiritual activity. Many men and women are painfully dissatisfied with their level of contact with God. "I just don't feel like I get through to Him very often" is a typical comment.

A disorganized spirit often means lack of inner serenity. For some, what should be tranquility is in fact only numbness or emptiness. Some suffer from restlessness, a feeling that they never quite measure up to the expectations they think God has for them. A common concern is the inability to maintain spiritual momentum, to have reasonably consistent attitudes and desires. "I start out my week with great intentions," a young person comments, "but by Wednesday morning, I've lost interest. I just can't sustain a spiritual life that is satisfying. So I get to the point where I'm tired of trying."

THE QUICK FIX

A look at the great saints of Scripture sometimes makes us envious. We reflect upon the burning-bush experience of Moses, Isaiah's vision in the temple, and the confrontation Paul had on the road to Damascus. Those were powerful starts to noble lives of spiritual vitality.

We are tempted to say, "If I could have had an experience like any of those, I'd be spiritually fixed for life." We assume our spirituality might be enhanced by some dramatic moment that would indelibly burn itself upon our consciousness. Were we to be impressed by such a spectacular touch with God, we would never – so we think – be tempted to doubt the matter again.

That is one reason many of us are tempted to reach out for a sort of "quick fix" that makes God seem real and more intimate. Some feel deeply enriched if they are caused to feel terribly guilty by a preacher who angrily thunders forth with accusations and denunciations. Others quest after emotional experiences that lift them out of themselves into ecstatic levels. Sometimes one looks about in a so-called contemporary worship service and wonders what is really happening as people get caught up in the rhythmic, unbelievably loud, repetitive music. Is it worship, or is it a hypnotic experience that simply helps one forget the difficulties or the routines of real life outside the building?

There are those who immerse themselves in endless rounds of Bible teaching and study, making the search for pure doctrine a way of finding satisfactory intimacy with God. Still others pursue spirituality through busyness in the church. Usually our choice of these or other ways of filling the seemingly empty spirit is based upon our psychological temperament – what most effectively touches us for the moment and makes us feel at peace.

But the fact is that the average person – like you and me – is not likely to have a great biblical confrontation; nor would we be satisfied by the dramatic experiences that happen to others. If we are ever to develop a spiritual life that gives contentment, it will be because we approach spiritual living as a discipline, much as the athlete trains his body for competition.

One thing is certain: If we do not choose to take on that discipline, there is the possibility of a day – as one came to Howard Rutledge – when we will regret that we had not undertaken the challenge.

CULTIVATING THE GARDEN

How shall we describe this centre, this inner spiritual territory where encounters are almost too sacred for words? Beyond theological propositions, we are forced to speak through a collection of metaphors.

David of the Psalms was thinking in metaphors when he imagined his inner spirit to be like a pasture where God, the Shepherd, led him as a lamb. In his metaphor, he longed for calm waters, green pastures, and tables loaded with food to be eaten in safety. This was a place, David fantasized, where the soul was restored.

The eighteenth-century Christian poet William Cowper used the metaphor of a quiet pool:

A life all turbulence and noise may seem
To him that leads it wise and to be praised,
But wisdom is a pearl with most success
Sought in still waters.

(from The Task, book 3)

For me the helpful metaphor for the inner spiritual centre has been a garden, a place of potent peace and tranquillity. This garden is a place where the Spirit of God comes to make self-disclosure, to share wisdom, to give affirmation or rebuke, to provide encouragement, and to give direction and guidance. When this garden is in proper order, it is a quiet place, and there is an absence of busyness, of defiling noise, of confusion.

The inner garden is a delicate place, and if not properly maintained it will be quickly overrun by intrusive undergrowth. God does not often walk in disordered gardens. And that is why inner gardens that are ignored are said to be empty.

That is exactly what Howard Rutledge was struggling with when the pressure was at its highest in "Heartbreak" prison. Total isolation, frequent beatings, and deteriorating health had made his world a hostile place. What resources did he have to draw upon that would sustain him? According to his own admission, he'd squandered opportunities earlier in life to store up strength and resolve in his inner garden. "I was too busy, too preoccupied," he says, "to spend one or two short hours a week thinking about the really important things." Nevertheless, what little he had from his childhood, he seized and developed. Suddenly, God was a very real and very important part of his existence.

Bringing order to the spiritual dimension of our private worlds is spiritual gardening. It is the careful cultivation of spiritual ground. The gardener turns up soil, pulls out unwanted growth, plans the use of the ground, plants seeds, waters and nourishes, and enjoys the harvests that result. All of this is what many have called spiritual discipline.

I love the words of Brother Lawrence, a reflective Christian of many centuries ago who used the metaphor of a chapel:

> It is not needful always to be in church to be with God. We make a chapel of our heart, to which we can from time to time withdraw to have gentle, humble, loving communion with Him. Everyone is able to have these familiar conversations with God. Some more, some less – He knows our capabilities. *Let us make a start. Perhaps He only waits for us to make one whole-hearted resolve.* Courage! We have but a short time to live. [italics added][2]

Let us begin soon, Brother Lawrence coaxes us; time is short! The discipline of the spirit must begin now.

PRIVILEGES WE CAN LOSE

Unless we make that start, we lose out on a number of privileges that God designed in order to make us fully alive. For example, we will never learn to enjoy the eternal and infinite perspective on reality that we were created to have. Our powers of judgment will be substantially curtailed.

David shows us a bit of the eternal perspective when he wrote of the "kings of the earth" launching movements and systems by which they intend to replace God (Ps. 2:2). David would have been intimidated by these kings and movements had he not had the perspective of an eternal and sovereign God, whom he pictures as sitting in the heavens laughing over all these futile machinations. The result? David was not given to fear, as some might have been if their eternal perspective was lacking.

If the spiritual centre of our private world goes undisciplined, a second privilege we will lack will be a vital, life-giving friendship with Christ. Again, David was very much aware of the loss of this kind of contact with his God when he sinned with Bathsheba. He could stand it just so long, and then, when confronted by the prophet, he went racing to God with a cry of confession and a plea for restoration. That intimacy simply meant too much to him.

A third privilege undisciplined spirits will lose is the fear of accountability to God. There will be a growing forgetfulness that all we are and have comes from His good hand, and we will fall into the rut of assuming it is all ours. This happened to Uzziah, king of Judah, who had had a great relationship with God and then let it lapse (2 Chron. 26). The result was a growth in pride that led to an embarrassing downfall. He began a hero; he ended the fool. The difference was the growing chaos and disorder in his inner garden.

Finally, a neglected, disordered spiritual centre usually means that we have little reserve or resolve for crisis moments such as failure, humiliation, suffering, the death of a loved one, or loneliness. This was Rutledge's desperate situation. How unlike Paul in the Roman jail: everyone had left him, for good or bad reasons; but he was sure he was not alone. And where did such assurance come from? It came from years of spiritual discipline, of inner gardening that produced a place where he and God could meet alone regardless of the hostility of the public world about him.

Letting the spiritual centre fall into disrepair means, fourth, that we lose the awareness of our real size in comparison to the Creator. And conversely, we forget our specialness and value before Him as His sons and daughters. Forgetting these things, we make the mistakes of the prodigal son and end up making a series of disastrous judgments that have painful consequences.

WHAT WILL IT TAKE?

When the inner garden is under cultivation and God's Spirit is present, harvests are regular events. The fruits? Things like courage, hope, love, endurance, joy, and lots of peace. Unusual capacities for self-control and the ability to discern evil and to ferret out truth are also reaped. As the writer of the Proverbs put it:

> For wisdom will enter your heart,
> And knowledge will be pleasant to your soul;
> Discretion will guard you,
> Understanding will watch over you,
> To deliver you from the way of evil,
> From the man who speaks perverse things.
>
> (Prov. 2:10)

Richard Foster quotes a favorite author of mine, Thomas Kelly:

> We feel honestly the pull of many obligations and try to fulfill them all. And we are unhappy, uneasy, strained, oppressed, and fearful we shall be shallow . . . We have hints that there is a way of life vastly richer and deeper than all this hurried existence, a life of unhurried serenity and peace and power. If only we could slip over into that Centre! . . . We have seen and known some people who have found this deep Centre of living, where the fretful calls of life are integrated, where No as well as Yes can be said with confidence.[3]

Kelly speaks to the point: if only we could slip over into that Centre!

Down through the centuries the Christian mystics were the ones who took spiritual discipline most seriously. They studied it, practiced it, and not infrequently – we can't ignore this – carried the disciplines to unhealthy and dangerous extremes. But they believed that there had to be regular experiences of withdrawal from routines and relationships to seek God in an inner garden. They were quick to tell us that church services and religious celebrations were far from adequate. A man or a woman had to develop a chapel, still waters, or a garden in the private world, they said. There was no alternative.

Jesus certainly pursued the discipline of His spirit. We know that David did. And so did Moses, the apostles, and Paul, who wrote of his own routines:

> I run in such a way, as not without aim; I box in such a way, as not beating the air; but I buffet my body and make it my slave, lest possibly, after I have preached to others, I myself should be disqualified. (1 Cor. 9:26-27)

Have we cheapened this spiritual discipline, this cultivation of the inner garden? Today Christians talk about the importance of "quiet time," a daily devotional often reduced to a system or method that is swift and streamlined. We boil it down to seven minutes or thirty minutes, depending on how much time we have available. We use Bible study guides, devotional guides, devotional booklets, and carefully organized prayer lists, all of which are nice – better, I suppose, than nothing – but not nearly as effective as what the mystics had in mind.

A major Christian magazine once called me to ask if I would spend a day with an outstanding Christian leader from another country who was visiting our city of Boston. They wanted me to lead him through an in-depth interview about himself, so that readers could gain insight into him as a person. I called on him to request permission for the conversation.

"And what shall we talk about?" he asked me.

"I thought we'd talk about your life as a preacher, a writer, and a scholar," I said. "Perhaps we could get into your views of family life, friendships, and your spiritual disciplines – "

"My spiritual disciplines?" he broke in.

"Yes," I came back. "A lot of people would love to know something of the ways in which you've pursued a personal walk with God."

I'll never forget his response.

"That part of my life is far too private to share with anyone."

I still think that many of us who are younger men and women in ministry would have profited from this older man's insights; nevertheless, I heard what he was trying to say. That part of his private world was just that: strictly private. It had been developed in a kind of secrecy, and it would stay that way. He and God would share it together – and alone. It would not be reduced to a system so that it could be adopted or imported into someone else's experience.

I have thought often about this man's reluctance to open his personal life at the depth I wished to explore. Perhaps it was because he was of another culture that he did not understand our American curiosity and our tendency to blab about everything that is personal to us even if it risks uncovering too much of ourselves. One does wonder if we have simply talked too much in our books and magazine articles – told each other too much when we should have reserved the conversation for God alone. Just a thought. At least one I need to think.

What will it take to force us into disciplined cultivation of the inner garden of our private worlds? Will it require an experience of severe suffering? That is what history seems to say over and over again: those under pressure seek God, because there is nothing else. Those smothered in "blessings" tend to drift with the current. And that is why I question the word blessing sometimes. Surely something is not a blessing if it seduces us away from inward spiritual cultivation.

Can the importance of the inward centre ever be appreciated until we have come close to death, defeat, or humiliation? But the command and the precedents come to us over and over again, in the Scriptures and through the history of the great saints. He who orders his inner spiritual world will make a place for God to visit and speak. And when that voice is heard, it will be unlike anything else ever spoken. That is what Howard Rutledge discovered. But it took a prisoner-of-war experience to force him to find it out.

Brother Lawrence says, "Let us make a start." Thomas Kelly admonishes: "Slip over into that Centre!" Jesus calls, "Come learn of Me." How does this discipline of the spirit happen?

MEMO TO THE DISORGANIZED

If my private world is in order, it will be because I am unafraid to be alone and quiet before Christ.

ELEVEN

No Outer Props Necessary

WHEN E. STANLEY JONES, METHODIST MISSIONARY TO India,was an aged man, he had a debilitating stroke that left him immobile and virtually speechless. But not faithless. "I need no outer props to hold up my faith," he wrote, "for my faith holds me." But he sadly saw that his was not the experience of everyone around him.

> I was talking to a bishop who had retired. He was frustrated. When he was no longer in the limelight of the bishopric, he was frustrated and told me so. He wanted to know the secret of victorious living. I told him it was in selfsurrender. *The difference was in giving up the innermost self to Jesus*. The difference was in the texture of the things that held him. When the outer strands were broken by retirement, the inner strands were not enough to hold him. Apparently he had a case of "limelight-itis" instead of a case of surrender to Jesus. *Fortunately, with me, surrender to Jesus was the primary thing, and when the outer strands were cut by this stroke, my life didn't shake.* [italics added][1]

Jones understood what Thomas Kelly is saying when he calls for us to slip over into the centre. Who of us would not like to have Jones's perspective and endurance? But how many of us are destined, due to neglect of our inner garden, to fall into the trap the bishop set for himself?

How do we cultivate the inner garden of our private worlds?

Because this book is not primarily a treatment of spiritual disciplines, I cannot survey all the ways the saints have found to strengthen the inner spirit. Instead, I have selected four spiritual exercises of critical importance, exercises that I find many Christ followers neglecting. They are: the pursuit of solitude and silence; regular listening to God; the experience of reflection and meditation; and prayer as worship and intercession.

SILENCE AND SOLITUDE

The desert fathers of centuries ago, Henri Nouwen tells us, understood the importance of a silent environment for the cultivation of the spirit when they called out to one another, "Fuge, terche, et quisset" – silence, solitude, and inner peace.

Few of us can fully appreciate the terrible conspiracy of noise there is about us, noise that denies us the silence and solitude we need for this cultivation of the inner garden. It would not be hard to believe that the archenemy of God has conspired to surround us at every conceivable point in our lives with the interfering noises of civilization that, when left unmuffled, usually drown out the voice of God. One who walks with God will tell you plainly, God does not ordinarily shout to make Himself heard. As Elijah discovered, God tends to whisper in the garden.

I recall a visit to a missionary centre in Latin America where workmen were constructing a sound studio for a radio station. They were taking careful measures to soundproof the rooms so that no noise from the city streets could mar the broadcasts and recordings that would emanate from that place. We must learn to soundproof the heart against the intruding noises of the public world in order to hear what God has to say. I love the words of Mother Teresa of Calcutta:

> We need to find God, and he cannot be found in noise and restlessness. *God is the friend of silence.* See how nature – trees, flowers, grass – grow in silence; see the stars, the moon and sun, how they move in silence . . . the more we receive in silent prayer, the more we can give in our active life. *We need silence to be able to touch souls.* The essential thing is not what we say, but what *God* says to us and through us. All our words will be useless unless they come from within – words which do not give the light of Christ increase the darkness. [italics added][2]

Our worlds are filled with the noise of endless music, chatter, and busy schedules. In most homes there is a stereo in almost every room, in every car, in each office, in the elevator. When I dial a friend at his office I am offered music over the phone until he comes to answer my call. There are cell phones with Beethoven's Ninth Symphony theme for a ring, Walkmans with mega-bass, and MP3s, all invading the mind with noise. Pretty noise, most of the time. But nevertheless noise. With the intrusion of so much noise, when can we withdraw and monitor the still, small voice of God?

We are so accustomed to noise that we grow restless without it. Worshipers in a congregation find it difficult to sit in quietness for more than a minute or two; we assume that something has gone wrong and someone has forgotten his assignment. Most of us would find it difficult to go even an hour without saying anything or hearing a word from someone.

The struggle can be the same in the experience of solitude. Not only are we often bothered by silence, but few of us are comfortable with times of aloneness. But there must be times of rhythmic withdrawal. There must be those moments when we break from routines, from other relationships, from the demands of the outer world to meet Him in the garden. It cannot be done in large meetings and spectacular celebrations.

Nouwen quotes Thomas Merton, a student of those strange mystics of the early Christian centuries who sometimes pursued solitude to an extreme. What he says about them is instructive. Why did they seek solitude?

> They knew that they were helpless to do any good for others as long as they floundered about in the wreckage [of humanity]. But once they got a foothold on solid ground, things were different. Then they had not only the power but even the obligation to pull the whole world to safety after them.[3]

It is interesting that God's angel used silence to curb the impossibility thinking of aged Zacharias when he found that he and his wife were to become the parents of John the Baptizer. If Zacharias could not accept the promise of God as it had come to him, then his tongue would be stilled for several months, and he could think about it. On the other hand, when Elizabeth, his wife, realized what was happening, she withdrew, the Scripture says, partially because that was the custom of pregnant women but also, I believe, because she needed to meditate upon the strange and mysterious things that were happening.

Then there was Mary, who, when she learned of her role in the birth of our Lord, did not blurt out all of God's plans, but chose silence. "Mary treasured up all these things, pondering them in her heart" (Luke 2:19). Christ's coming was heralded not only by singing and praise from angels but also by silence from human partners who needed solitude in order to think through and appreciate the wonder.

Wayne Oates tells us,

> Silence is not native to my world. Silence, more than likely, is a stranger to your world, too. If you and I

ever have silence in our noisy hearts, we are going to
have to grow it . . . You can nurture silence in your
noisy heart if you value it, cherish it, and are eager to
nourish it.[4]

Silence and solitude have not come easily to me at all. I
once equated them with laziness, inaction, and a lack of
productivity. The minute I was alone, my mind
exploded with a list of things I should do: phone calls to
make, papers I should be filing, books unread, sermons
unprepared, and people I ought to see.

The slightest noise outside my study door was a
massive intrusion to concentration. It seemed as if my
hearing became supersensitive, and I could overhear
conversations at the other end of our house. My
curiosity strained to hear what was being said. Because
my study was, for years, near our laundry room, it never
seemed to fail that the moment I got into spiritual
activity the washing machine would decide the load
inside was unbalanced, and its foghorn-like buzzer
would go off, insisting that I, since everyone else was
upstairs, should come and readjust the wash.

But concentrating even when there was silence
became desperately difficult. I learned that I had to
warm up, to accept the fact that for about fifteen
minutes my mind would do everything it could to resist
the solitude. So among the things I did was to start by
reading or writing on the subject of my spiritual
pursuits. Slowly, it seemed, my conscious mind got the
message: We (my mind and I) were going to worship
and meditate, and the sooner the mind got in touch
with the inner garden on the matter, the better it would
be.

I expect that I will fight this battle of solitude and
silence for as long as I live. I want to say, however, that as
time has gone by, and I have begun to reap the benefits
of silent time, there has been a growing hunger for
more of it. But still there is that first resistance to be

overcome. When one is an activist by nature, withdrawal can be hard work. But it is a necessary labour.

For me that silence and solitude is best found in the early morning hours. So it goes in that spot on my calendar before anyone can suggest other purposes for the time. For others, it may be late in the evening. But anyone wanting to bring order to the spiritual sector of the private world must find the place and the time that fits his personal temperament.

LISTENING TO GOD

It must have been like a cold shower on an early morning for Moses when he came off the mountain after having been with God and found his Hebrew people dancing around a golden calf. For days he had lived in the presence of holiness itself, and a sense of God's glory and righteousness had been burned into his spirit. But now this spectacle! He was heartbroken.

How had it happened? While Moses had been listening to God, his brother, Aaron, high priest of all the people, had been listening to the people. The input the two received was decidedly different. When Moses listened, he received God's revelation of the law of righteousness. When Aaron listened, he heard complaints, wishes, and demands. Moses brought with him uncompromised standards of heaven; Aaron caved in to the whims of men. It was all in the listening.

The garden of our private worlds is cultivated not only when we draw apart for times of silence and solitude, but also when we begin, in that environment, to deliberately practice the discipline of listening. I have not met many who know how to listen to God. Busy people find it hard to learn how. Most Christians learned at an early age how to talk to God, but they did not learn to listen as well.

We listen every time we open the Scriptures and place ourselves at the feet of the inspired writers who unfold the mysteries of God. We listen, as I shall point out later on, when we sensitize ourselves to the proddings of God's indwelling Holy Spirit. Listening happens when the preacher or teacher of Scripture, empowered by God's Spirit, brings instruction.

All these things are worth discussing (not to mention doing!). But right now I would like to talk about another exercise, one that can form a base for all the other ways of listening.

• Journal Keeping – A Way to Listen to God

When I studied some of the mystic and contemplative Christians, I found that one practical way to learn to listen to God speak in the garden of my private world was to keep a journal. With a pencil in hand ready to write, I found that there was an expectancy, a readiness to hear anything God might wish to whisper through my reading and reflection.

That discovery came almost thirty-five years ago, while I was reading a biography. The subject of the book had maintained a lifelong habit of recording his spiritual pilgrimage. I was now benefiting from that discipline, even though he had been writing more for his own benefit than for mine. As he had been tutored by God's Spirit, he had kept careful notes. What a tool that must have been – something to go back to again and again and trace the hand of God upon his life.

I became impressed by the fact that many, many godly men and women down through the centuries had also kept journals, and I began to wonder if they had not put their fingers upon an aid to spiritual growth. To satisfy my curiosity, I decided to experiment and began keeping one for myself.

At first it was difficult. I felt self-conscious. I was worried that I would lose the journal or that someone might peek inside to see what I'd said. But slowly the self-consciousness began to fade, and I found myself recording in the journal more and more of the thoughts that flooded my inner spirit. Into the journal went words describing my feelings, my fear and sense of weakness, my hopes, and my discoveries about where Christ was leading me. When I felt empty or defeated, I talked about that too in the journal.

Slowly I began to realize that the journal was helping me come to grips with an enormous part of my inner person that I had never been fully honest about. No longer could fears and struggles remain inside without definition. They were surfaced and named. And I became aware, little by little, that God's Holy Spirit was directing many of the thoughts and insights as I wrote. On paper, I felt that God and I were carrying on a personal communion. He was helping me, in the words of David, to "search my heart." He was prodding me to put words to my fears, shapes to my doubts. And when I was candid about it, then there would often come out of Scripture or from the meditations of my own heart the reassurances, the rebukes, and the admonishments that I so badly needed. But this began to happen only when the journal was employed.

Because I found that my prayers often seemed disconnected and that I was not able to concentrate (or even stay awake), I often wondered if I could ever develop a vigorous worship and intercessory life. Again, the journal provided a vehicle for writing prayers when my spoken prayers lacked cohesiveness. Now prayer content became sensible, and I began to enjoy recording my progress as a believer and a follower of Christ.

A key contribution of the journal became its record of not only the good moments, but the bad times as well. When there came times of discouragement, even of despair, I was able to describe my feelings and tell how

God's Spirit ultimately ministered to me to strengthen my resolve. These became special passages to look back upon; they helped me celebrate the power of God in the midst of my own weakness.

I am reminded that the Lord once had the Israelites save "three quarts of manna" (Ex. 16:33 tlb) so that they would have a tangible reminder of His constant care. The journal became my "three quarts," for in it I had all the testimony I needed to the faithfulness of God in my life. This remembering process, which a journal provides, is very significant.

Today, after thirty-five years of journal keeping, I have acquired the journalist's habit. Hardly a morning passes that I do not open the journal and record the things I hear God saying through my reading, meditation, and daily experience. When the journal opens, so does the ear of my heart. If God is going to speak, I am ready to listen.

When W. E. Sangster was a young pastor in England, he grew increasingly restive about the spiritual climate in the English Methodist church. Brooding upon his own role in future leadership, he turned to his journal to sharpen his thinking. In it he could lay out his innermost thoughts and meditations on paper and perceive what God was laying on his heart. Reading his thoughts several decades later reveals how one man used a journal to bring order to his private world so that he could later be used to press order into his outer world. One day he wrote:

> I feel a commission to work under God for the revival of this branch of His Church – careless of my own reputation; indifferent to the comments of older and jealous men. I am thirty-six. If I am to serve God in this way, I must no longer shrink from the task – but do it.

I have examined my heart for ambition. I am certain it is not there. I hate the criticism I shall evoke and the painful chatter of people. Obscurity, quiet browsing among books, and the service of simple people is my taste – but by the will of God, this is my task . . .

Bewildered and unbelieving, I heard the voice of God saying to me, "I want to sound the note through you." O God, did ever an apostle shrink from his task more? I dare not say "No" but, like Jonah, I would fain [wish to] run away.

God help me. God help me. What is the initial task? To call Methodism back to its real work.[5]

Sangster's words offer a beautiful example of a man listening to God in his private world through the use of a journal. He put his dreams on paper in order to separate destructive ambition from genuine call. He searched for hints that his thoughts were not those of his heavenly Father. He wrestled with self-doubt. Isn't it interesting that, as he perceived the divine whisper, he transformed into print the still, small voice of his Lord?

• How to Journal

When I have spoken in public on "journaling," I have found that people are intensely interested and have many questions. Their initial curiosity tends to centre on technique more than anything else. What does your journal look like? How often do you write in it? What sorts of things do you include? Isn't it really just a diary? Do you let your wife read your journal? Although I am by no means an expert journal keeper, I endeavor to answer as best I can.

For many years my journals were simple spiral-bound notebooks that I purchased at an office-supply store. They were rather unimpressive in appearance. I was able to fill one of them with about three months of writing. Many years later, in the age of personal computers, I began to write my journal to a disk. Now when I finish a month of writing, I print out the pages, accumulate them until I have about two hundred pages and then take them to a place like Staples or Office Depot where they spiral-bind them and give them an attractive cover.

I write in my journal almost every day, but I am not overly concerned if an occasional day passes without an entry. I have made it a habit to write in the earliest moments of my time of spiritual exercise, and for me that means the first thing in the morning.

So what might you find in my journal? An account of things that I accomplished in the preceding day, people I met, things I learned, feelings I experienced, and impressions I believe God wanted me to have.

In days past, I wrote of our children as they grew up in our home. The stories of their athletic activities, their first dates, when they got their driver's licenses, the various graduations: they're all there. Our intimate conversations, my dreams and worries about them, my unbounded delight in their growth in character: that's there too. And now the journals say a lot about grandchildren who have come along to bless my life.

As I said before, I include prayers if I feel like writing them down, insights that come from reading the Bible and other spiritual literature, and concerns I have about my own personal behavior. I love to record things I am seeing in the lives of members of my family. I anticipate that someday our children and grandchildren will read through some of these journals, and if I can posthumously affirm them for things I see in their growing lives today, it will be a treasure for them.

All of this is part of listening to God. As I write, I am aware that what I am writing may actually be what God wants to tell me. I dare to presume that His Spirit is often operative in the things I am choosing to think about and record. And it becomes important to search my heart to see what conclusions He may be engendering, what matters He wishes to remind me about, what themes He hopes to stamp upon my private world.

Occasionally someone asks, "What would an entry in your journal sound like?" I'm not overly comfortable opening up my journal for others to examine. Many of its pages are rather private, you understand. But I did look through my most recent journal writings and came up with this sample for those who are constructively curious.

> I find myself dreading the 6 a.m. news each morning because the world is in such terrible shape right now. I think back two years ago when we dared to dream that the Israeli/Palestinian conflict just might be headed toward resolution. But today! I can hardly remember any moment when things have been worse, when the two sides hated each other more. What a terrible, terrible waste of human life. An entire generation of children and young people being raised to hate. Please, Father: divine intervention!

> My Bible reading this morning is from Matthew 6. The first half of the chapter focuses on giving and praying. All to be done, basically, in secret. Nothing designed to impress anybody. Clearly, Jesus is disturbed by the tendency then (and now?) to make a big deal out of these religious disciplines so that the effort becomes something intended to impress people more than to align one's heart with God.

> "Be careful not to do your 'acts of righteousness' before men, to be seen by them." I've been thinking while reading this about our habit of self-analysis, something a tad different from self-examination. Not only are we tempted to "perform" for others, but we sometimes perform for ourselves. Even as I pray, for example, I sometimes find myself analyzing the quality of my own prayer. Does it sound "saintly" enough? Could I have said it better?

Even as I give or serve, I sometimes find myself watching and critiquing myself, wondering how it comes across to others. Such is the complexity of spiritual life, the garbledness of so much we do. I'm challenged once again to assure that my motives and purposes are examined for unsoundness.

I must be sure that Gail knows how much I appreciate her attentiveness to me over the last few days. We have had some wonderful laughs together. Yesterday we spent a couple of hours cleaning up winter debris in the front field. She raked, and I put the leaves and sticks through the chipper. Now Gail has plenty of stuff for her mulching operation. She was delighted. Not hard to make her happy. This year I'm committed to liking yard work more.

My journal also becomes a repository of quotes and insights that come from my Bible reading and the books I am going through at the time. If a comment by an author stands out, I like to copy it into the journal (in boldface) so that the very exercise of typing it out stamps it more deeply into my mind. It is a fascinating experience to occasionally page back through a journal from a year or two ago and see all the thoughts that I'd place in there that were influencing me at that moment.

Thumbing through my most recent journal I find a stirring excerpt from Peter Alexander's biography of Alan Paton, the great South African author. Speaking of the critical moment in Paton's life when he saw with clarity the horror of apartheid and his own sense of call to fight it, Alexander wrote:

Finding a way to reconcile (black nationalists and Afrikaners) was to be the task of Paton's life, and it was during the war that he dedicated himself to it. The prize for success would be the peace of his country; the price of failure he would not even contemplate. The task might prove impossible, but he was going to give his whole heart to it.[6]

My journals are not heavy with merely serious spiritual reflections or intellectual musings. They are also a place where I enjoy recording the light things of life.

> The baseball season has started today, and the Red Sox have lost their first game to Toronto. Pedro Martinez was humiliated for 7 or 8 runs and an unthinkable number of hits. The NCAA championship game was played last evening, and Gail and I sat up and watched it. Maryland over Indiana! And, believe it or not, the Patriots have begun early season workouts. Do I have to start worrying about defending the Super Bowl championship this soon? So the world plays while the Middle East heats up and unravels.

The pile of these journals (now in the many dozens) continues to grow. Fearful that they might get lost if there was ever a fire in our home, Gail went out and purchased a fireproof safe so that these volumes that she and I have kept (Gail is also a journaler) will survive a disaster.

Does Gail read my journals? I suppose she has occasionally taken a look. After forty years of marriage, I really couldn't care less. Our relationship is quite intimate enough that there is little in there that would surprise her now.

To those who are concerned about a potential lack of privacy in such matters, I suggest that they simply find a place where the journal could be locked up and kept from those you would rather not have see inside. If confidentiality is important, you should be able to find a way to maintain it. Concern for privacy is not an adequate reason for not attempting a journal.

Journal keeping becomes a habit for most people if they will stick with it for the better part of a year. Most people quit too quickly, never achieving the habit pattern, and that is unfortunate.

I am careful to keep a journal even when I am traveling. It helps me to maintain a record of those I have met, so that when I return again to places where I have visited, I can simply review my previous visit in the journal and pick up relationships where they may have been suspended due to distance.

Since I first wrote about journaling, it has been fascinating to me to see how many people have written books about the subject. One could probably go to any religious bookstore and find several dozen books about keeping a journal. When I have leafed through some of them, I've been disappointed with those who tried to reduce this effort – as in a lot of spiritual disciplines – to systems and gimmickry. But on the other hand, the proliferation of literature on journaling suggests that more and more people are seeking a way to gain perspective and meaning on lives caught up in a torrent of demands, noises, and distractions. If a journal can help to give shape to a quiet period in one's daily life, then let it be so.

Looking back on my thirty-five years of journaling, I can tell you that establishing the discipline was among the most important decisions of my life. I have a record of the faithfulness of God, the greatest and the darkest moments of my life, the story of my family and my friends, the tidbits from innumerable books. The dozens of journals that sit in that safe are wealth to me.

My mind goes back to Howard Rutledge in his prison camp. Every voice was a hostile one; every noise introduced the possibility of something about to go wrong. In such an ugly place, was there a friendly voice, a lovely sound to be heard anywhere? Yes, if you have trained your ears to hear in the inner garden. There the greatest of all sounds may be heard: those belonging to Him who seeks our companionship and growth. In the words of an old and very sentimental hymn:

He speaks, and the sound of his voice
Is so sweet the birds hush their singing.

(C. Austin Miles, "In the Garden")

NO OUTER PROPS NECESSARY

MEMO TO THE DISORGANIZED

If my private world is in order, it will be because I absorb the words of Christ into my attitudes and actions.

TWELVE

Everything Has to Be Entered

ON HIS DEATHBED, IN GREAT DISCOMFORT, AND BARELY able to communicate, E. Stanley Jones managed to dictate some final thoughts that summed up his Christian journey. Employing the metaphor of a mountain climber's rope to describe the toughness of his spirit, he said, "The innermost strands are the strongest. I need no outer props to hold up my faith, for my faith holds me." Noble words, these. Worth one's pause and reflection.

Despite such courage, Jones would have been the first to acknowledge that it had not always been that way. In the early days of his life and ministry there had come a temporary sinkhole collapse. For more than a year he had languished in both spiritual and physical ineffectiveness. "The spiritual sag brought on a physical sag," he remembered. "The outer collapse took place because the inner experience could not sustain it. I had made it a life motto that I would not preach what I was not experiencing, so the outer and the inner came together in collapse."[1]

When an old saint – now with the Lord – makes it a point to recall difficult days on the spiritual journey, it's time to listen. He offers a caution to younger men and women. He is telling us that no matter how good life might be at any one moment, tests of the "inner strands" are only a matter of time. Jones and people like him who finished their lives with great spiritual strength did not get that way by simply staying busy. They understood the priority of spiritual discipline.

The discipline of the spirit – what I have called the cultivation of the inner garden – depends upon the willingness of men and women of Christ to seek solitude and silence and to listen for the whisper of God.

But the things that we hear in solitude and silence must be internalized. Years ago, when I wrote the first edition of Ordering Your Private World, a lot of us were just beginning to become familiar with the personal computer. Bravely, I bought one of the first IBM PCs, thinking it would revolutionize my way of writing and of storing and retrieving information I needed for sermons and books. But figuring out how to use the computer was a huge task. No one really knew how the things worked. Even the salesman who sold me the bulky machine and printer (for $7200) could barely describe how to switch it on, let alone boot up the word processing program. I would have to find out for myself.

It took me almost three weeks to figure out how to use the computer even in the most basic sense. One of the first things I had to get used to was the function of the "enter" key. The teaching manual instructed me that I could type anything I wanted on the screen in front of me. But until I hit the "enter" key, the computer would not "hear" or respond to a single word I had typed. All of my words, no matter how impressive, would just sit on the screen's surface until I entered them onto a file in the heart (the "memory") of the computer.

It occurred to me that this was not unlike my listening processes, for I have the ability to hear things but that does not necessarily mean that everything enters or penetrates my heart.

Salvation Army Commissioner Samuel Logan Brengle, speaking of his spiritual disciplines, wrote:

> I do a lot of listening. Prayer, you know, is not meant to be a monologue, but a dialogue. It is a communion, a friendly talk. While the Lord communicates with me mainly through His Word, he gives me a great deal of comfort in a direct manner. By "comfort" I do not mean cuddling or coddling, but assurance – assurance of His presence with me and His pleasure in my service. It is like the comfort given by a military commander to his soldier or envoy whom he sends on a difficult mission: "You go, put on your armor, I'm watching you, and I'll send you all the reinforcements you need as they are needed." I have to be comforted that way a great deal. I don't just assume that God is near me and pleased with me; I must have a fresh witness daily.[2]

The Bible tells of another Samuel, a young boy interning in the tabernacle under the discipleship of Eli, the high priest. In the night Samuel heard a voice calling his name. Running to Eli's bed, he assumed that he was being summoned for some task. But Eli had not called, and Samuel returned to his room. But the call came again and again. It was Eli who put things together and suggested how Samuel could respond the next time. "When you hear the voice again, Samuel, respond with these words: 'Speak, Lord, for your servant hears!'" In others words, Samuel, push the "enter" key.

Samuel did, and God spoke. The words of God penetrated his heart and changed his destiny. We strengthen the innermost strands, as Jones put it, by making sure that God's words are entering the garden of our private worlds. Our first step in spiritual discipline is finding solitude and silence; the second step is learning to listen to God. The third step, the pushing of the "enter" key, is done through reflection and meditation.

Some Christians are uneasy and negative about the mention of such words. They think such practices can open a door to activity that is too undirected and that can lead to misguided conclusions. They conjure up images of people sitting in lotus positions and engaging in trancelike activities.

But the Bible is full of reflective or meditative passages and calls us to open our private worlds to them. Among the most popular are those passages out of the Psalms where the writer fixes his mind upon certain aspects of God's being and consistent care for His children.

The psalmist looked through all sorts of meditative lenses. For example, he saw God as a shepherd, as a commanding general, as a director of spiritual exercise.

The act of meditation is like tuning the spirit to heavenly frequencies. One takes a portion of Scripture and simply allows it to enter into the deepest recesses of self. There are often several different results: cleansing, reassurance, the desire to praise and give thanksgiving. Sometimes meditation on something of God's nature or His actions opens the mind to new guidance or a new awareness of something the Lord may be trying to say to us.

In his book of prayers, John Baillie reveals a meditational mood when he prays:

> Almighty God, in this quiet hour I seek communion with thee. From the fret and fever of the day's business, from the world's discordant noises, from the praise and blame of men, from the confused thoughts and vain imaginations of my own heart, I would now turn aside and seek the quietness of thy presence. All day long have I toiled and striven; but now in the stillness of heart and the clear light of

thine eternity, I would ponder the pattern my life is weaving.[3]

Meditation, of course, can be done only when we have chosen an environment where there will be adequate amounts of time, silence, and privacy. One does not get much meditation done on a bus or when driving in traffic – although I have heard people claim that was their time for the spiritual discipline.

Many of us will discover that it takes preparatory time in order to meditate. You may have had the experience of coming in from heavy exercise still breathing very hard. You know that it is virtually impossible to sit down for several minutes and be still. There is too much gasping and catching of breath for quiet sitting. The same is true in reflection. We often enter the chamber to meet with God while we are still emotionally out of breath. It is hard at first to concentrate our thoughts and to bring them into the presence of the Lord. We have to quietly relax for a short season while the mind accustoms itself to spiritual activity in the "garden" environment. Thus, it will take time – time some people are reluctant to give.

Christians have always considered the Bible to be the central revelation of our faith and worthy of meditation. Let me add that reading the great classics of Christian literature is a must for spiritual growth. Down through the centuries there have been men and women who have recorded their insights and exercises for us to read. And although these books do not carry the authoritative power of the Bible itself, they nevertheless contain an enormous amount of spiritual food.

Reflection and meditation demand a certain amount of imagination. We read the first psalm, for example, and picture a tree planted by a river. What is true about that tremendous tree to which the writer likens the man or woman who walks after God? In Psalm 19 we let our minds sweep across the universe and imagine the celestial bodies and their incredible message. When we read the passages describing Jesus' ministry, our reflecting minds place ourselves right into the story. We see the Saviour heal, hear Him teach, and respond to His directives. In meditation we latch on to phrases from the prophets, perhaps memorizing small portions, and we allow the words to trickle down over the structures of our inner being as we repeat them over and over again. From such exercises come new and wonderful conclusions. The word of God is *entering* our private worlds. And because we have fixed our attention upon His word, we can be sure the Holy Spirit will guide our meditations.

C. S. Lewis, writing to an American friend, spoke of reflective exercises:

> We all go through periods of dryness in our prayers, don't we? I doubt whether they are necessarily a bad symptom. I sometimes suspect that what we feel to be our best prayers are really our worst; that what we are enjoying is the satisfaction of apparent success, as in executing a dance or reciting a poem. Do our prayers sometimes go wrong because we insist on trying to talk to God when He wants to talk with us? Joy tells me that once, years ago, she was haunted one morning by a feeling that God wanted something of her, a persistent pressure like the nag of a neglected duty. And till mid-morning she kept on wondering what it was. But the moment she stopped worrying, the answer came through as plain as a spoken voice. It was "I don't want you to do anything. I want to give you something"; and immediately her heart was peace and delight. St. Augustine says, "God gives where He finds empty hands." A man whose hands are full of parcels can't receive a gift. Perhaps these parcels are not always sins or earthly cares, but sometimes our own fussy attempts to worship Him in *our* way. Incidentally, what most often interrupts my own prayers is not

great distractions but tiny ones – things one will have to do or avoid in the course of the next hour.[4]

Here is a good example of the exercise of reflection and meditation. God speaks; we listen, and the message is entered within the heart. The need for outer props is lessened; the inner garden is further cultivated. The man or woman of spiritual discipline is growing strong in the private world.

MEMO TO THE DISORGANIZED

If my private world is in order, it will be because I have begun to pursue the discipline of seeing events and people through the eyes of Christ so that my prayers reflect my desire to be in alignment with His purposes and promises for them.

THIRTEEN

Seeing Through Heaven's Eyes

IN AN INSIGHTFUL LITTLE BOOK ON CONTEMPLATIVE FAITH written more than sixty years ago, a European Christian by the name of Bridget Herman wrote:

> When we read the lives of the saints, we are struck by a certain large leisure which went hand in hand with a remarkable effectiveness. They were never hurried; they did comparatively few things, and these not necessarily striking or important; and they troubled very little about their influence. Yet they always seemed to hit the mark; every bit of their life told; their simplest actions had a distinction, an exquisiteness which suggested the artist. The reason is not far to seek. Their sainthood lay in their habit of referring the smallest actions to God. They lived in God; they acted from a pure motive of love towards God. They were as free from self-regard as from slavery to the good opinion of others. God saw and God rewarded: what else needed they? They possessed God and possessed themselves in God. Hence the inalienable dignity of these meek, quiet figures that seem to produce such marvelous effects with such humble materials.[1]

The fourth way we can enhance communion with God in the garden of our private worlds is through prayer as worship and intercession. This is what Bridget Herman says characterized the saints. "Their sainthood lay in their habit of referring the smallest actions to God."

"Let inward prayer be your last act before you fall asleep and the first act when you awake," Thomas Kelly wrote. "And in time you will find as did Brother Lawrence, that 'those who have the gale of the Holy Spirit go forward even in sleep.'"[2]

Most of us have never experienced this. Daily, disciplined prayer is one of the most difficult exercises Christians undertake.

Married men will often admit, for example, that praying with their wives is a very difficult thing. Why? They really don't have an answer. Sometimes pastors in a moment of self-revelation will reveal that the integrity of their prayer life is usually an embarrassment to them. And they also are hard pressed to explain it.

My impression after visiting with many Christians is that worship and intercession rank at the top of any list of spiritual struggles. No one would deny that prayer is important; but few believe their prayer life to be adequately developing. And this is a major reason the inner gardens of so many private worlds are in a state of disorder. It is why most of us would have a hard time saying, like E. Stanley Jones, "No outer props are necessary."

WHY WE HAVE TROUBLE PRAYING

Why do so many people have struggles when it comes to prayer? Let me suggest three possible reasons.

- ### Worship and Intercession Seem to Be Unnatural Acts

Men and women were originally created to desire communion with God. But the effects of sin have dulled most of that original human desire. Sin turned a natural activity into an unnatural function.

My suspicion is that when sin affected man so deeply, it touched his spiritual dimensions most severely of all, while leaving the original physical appetites and desires virtually undiminished. Our instinctive preoccupations with food, sexual pleasure, and security are probably close to their original levels. It may be helpful to speculate that man in his sinless nature once probably had as great, if not greater, desire for communion with the Creator as he has for the satisfaction of the natural and very real appetites and instincts that we live with today. But the spiritual hunger, once undoubtedly powerful, has been terribly dulled by the power of sin. Thus, worship and intercession have become difficult challenges.

As a result, praying in any meaningful way goes against virtually everything within our natural selves and is foreign to what our culture teaches us as a way of life.

And that is the heart of the trouble. Few people realize how brainwashed each of us is. Messages bombard our private worlds every day, telling us that anything of a spiritual nature is really a waste of time. From our earliest years we are subtly taught that the only way to achieve anything is through action. But prayer seems to be a form of inaction. To the person with a disordered private world, it does not seem to accomplish anything.

Until we believe that prayer is indeed a real and highly significant activity, that it does in fact reach beyond space and time to the God who is actually there, we will never acquire the habits of worship and intercession. In order to gain these habits, we must make a conscious effort to overcome the part of us that thinks that praying is not a natural part of life.

- **Worship and Intercession Are Tacit Admissions of Weakness**

A second reason people find it difficult to enter into worship and intercession is that these acts are by nature admissions of personal weakness. In the acts of prayer, something within the inner garden acknowledges that we are utterly dependent upon the One to whom we address our words.

Now we can say that we are weak people, and we can say that we depend upon God for all of our sustenance; but the fact is that something deep within us is not willing to *recognize* it. There is something deep within that vigorously denies our dependence.

As I mentioned earlier, I have often been fascinated with the reluctance of many Christian men to pray with their wives, or to feel free to take prayer leadership in a mixed group. It is not unusual for a Christian wife to complain, "My husband never prays with me, and I can't understand it."

The answer may lie in the fact that men have been taught in our culture never to reveal weakness or to engage in any activity that may show it. Prayer in its most authentic form acknowledges that we are weak and dependent upon our God. Something in the male knows this and unconsciously fights having to identify with the fact of dependence.

On the other hand, it is my observation that most women, at least until recently, have never had to struggle to face their own weaknesses; and that may be one reason that, as a group, they feel more at ease in prayer than men. Generalizations, these, of course. But may I be frank? The generalizations about men and women at prayer are pretty consistent.

A person shows significant spiritual growth when he finds it possible to admit that he needs a relationship with God in order to be the human being he was created to be. There is an enormous sense of liberation in that realization.

Brother Lawrence wrote:

> We must examine with care what are the virtues of which we stand most in need, what are those which are most difficult to win, the sins to which we most often fall, and the most frequent and inevitable occasions of our falling. We must turn to God in complete confidence in the hour of battle, abide strongly in the presence of his divine majesty, worship him humbly, and set before him our woes and our weaknesses. And thus we shall find in him all virtues though we may lack them all.[3]

Brother Lawrence seemed never to have any problems facing up to his weaknesses, and that is one reason his prayer life was so alive.

- **Prayer Sometimes Seems to Be Unrelated to Actual Result**

A third reason prayer comes hard to us is the fact that it seems frequently unrelated to actual results. Lest you think I am guilty of denying a substantial teaching of Scripture, hear me carefully. I do in fact believe that God answers prayer. But most of us have had enough experience to realize that His answers do not always come in forms or on schedules that we would have designed.

As a very young pastor, I recall acknowledging my confusion about this matter of personal prayer to my wife. "Sometimes it seems as if, on those weeks when I pray very little, my sermons come out very powerful. And on those weeks when I feel that I've really done my prayer work, I seem to preach my worst. Now you tell me," I'd challenge her, "what does God expect me to do when He doesn't seem to give me, pound for pound, the blessings that match my prayer investment?"

Like others, I have prayed for healings, for miracles, for guidance, and for assistance. Frankly, there were times I was sure God would answer me because I had mustered strong feelings of faith. But many of those times nothing happened – or if it did, it was entirely unlike what I had anticipated.

We live in a society that is reasonably organized. Put a letter in the box, and it usually ends up where you want it to go. Order an item on the Internet, and it usually comes to you in the right size, color, and model. Ask someone to provide you a service, and it is reasonable to expect that it will work out that way. In other words, we are used to results in response to our arrangements. That is why prayer can be discouraging for some of us. How can we predict the result? We are tempted to abandon prayer as a viable exercise and to try getting the results ourselves.

But the fact is that my prayer life cannot be directly tied to the results I expect or demand. I have had many opportunities by now to see that the things I want God to do in response to my prayers can be unhealthy for me. I have begun to see that worship and intercession are far more the business of aligning myself with God's purposes than asking Him to align with mine.

Henri Nouwen said it best when he once wrote:

> Prayer is a radical conversion of all our mental processes because in prayer we move away from ourselves, our worries, preoccupation, and self-gratification – and direct all that we recognize as ours to God in the simple trust that through his love all will be made new.[4]

When our Lord came to the garden on the night of His crucifixion, His prayer just before His capture centered on affirming His oneness with the Father's purposes. This is mature praying.

Many times I have gone to prayer with results in mind. I wanted to gain control over the people and events I was praying about by dictating to the Father my views on how things should come out. When I do this, I am looking at people and events through an earthly lens and not a heavenly one. I am praying as though I know better than God what is best for the outcome.

Thomas Kelly suggests that a more proper kind of prayer is, "Lord, be Thou my will." Perhaps among the purest prayers we can pray is simply to ask, "Father, may I see earth through heaven's eyes."

Again Kelly wrote:

> The life that intends to be wholly obedient, wholly submissive, wholly listening, is astonishing in its completeness. Its joys are ravishing, its peace profound, its humility the deepest, its power world shaking, its love enveloping, its simplicity that of a trusting child.[5]

It was this kind of thinking that helped me overcome the obstacles to worship and intercession that have often been quite real to me. Yes, praying is unnatural for the natural man. But Christ has entered life, and what once was unnatural now becomes natural if I ask for the power to make it so. Yes, praying signals weakness and dependence. But that is the truth about me, and I am healthier for coming to grips with it. And yes, the answers to my prayers do not always coincide with my expectations. But the problem is in my expectations – not in the capacities or sensitivities of God.

Having encountered these obstacles, how do we develop the discipline of worship and intercession in the garden?

VISITING WITH GOD

The practical side of worship and intercession has to do with time – when to pray; posture – how to pray; and content – what to include during visits with the Father.

All of us will find different parts of the day best for our spiritual disciplines. I am a morning person; but one of my closest friends tells me that he finds the evening hours best. Whereas I begin the day in prayer, he ends it that way. Neither of us has airtight arguments for his choice; I think it is a matter of individual rhythms. Daniel of Babylon solved the problem by being a morning and an evening person – and a noontime person too.

When I come to the morning hour, I find it virtually impossible to enter into worship or intercession the moment I come to my private place of solitude. Remember the out-of-breath principle? Praying with a fully active mind fresh from a host of conversations and decisions is difficult, if not impossible. To pray meaningfully, the mind has to be slowed down to a reflective pace.

In order to make this happen, I often begin by reading or writing in my journal. This sort of thing will slowly convince my mind that I am really serious about spiritual exercise, and so it is less liable to rebel when I turn toward prayer.

Is there a prime posture for prayer? Probably not, although some would like to make us think so. In the biblical cultures, people were most likely to stand while they prayed. However the very word *prayer* from the Old Testament means to prostrate oneself, and that may mean at times full length upon the floor.

Friends of A. W. Tozer, a great man of prayer in our time, tell me that he had a pair of coveralls in the closet in his study. When he came to the moments of prayer in his day, he put them on and stretched out upon the hard floor. The coveralls, of course, prevented him from getting his dress clothes dirty. Although one or two may find it out of place to say this, the fact is that the Muslim posture for prayer is worth trying. This is done by kneeling and then leaning forward until one's forehead is touching the floor. I have found that when I am tired, the Muslim posture helps me to be mentally and spiritually alert.

Sometimes I pray while pacing back and forth in my study; on other occasions I am content simply to sit. The point is that prayer can be carried on in all different postures – and perhaps it is best to assume all of them from one time to another.

Serious intercessors keep prayer lists. Although I am not implying that I call myself a serious intercessor, I do keep one, usually on index cards that I can keep close to me. They help me to review my chief concerns as I pray. It's the only way I know of making sure that those for whom God has given me a burden are responsibly lifted up as an expression of my love and caring.

THE CONTENT OF PRAYER

That should we pray about? Take a look at an excerpt from the prayers of Samuel Logan Brengle, an evangelist of the Salvation Army at the beginning of our century:

> Keep me, O Lord, from waxing mentally and spiritually dull and stupid. Help me to keep the physical, mental, and spiritual fiber of the athlete, of the man who denies himself daily and takes up his cross and follows Thee. Give me good success in my work, but hide pride from me. Save me from the self-complacency that so frequently accompanies success and prosperity. Save me from the spirit of

sloth, of self-indulgence, as physical infirmities and decay creep upon me.[6]

No wonder Brengle was effective. He knew how and what to pray for. There was nothing held back, even in a short piece of intercession like this one. Having recorded this prayer, Brengle's biographer adds: "Thus praying daily and hourly, the prophet kept his passion hot and his eye single, even as he came down the decline."

Adoration

In our spiritual disciplines when we visit with the Father in the inner garden, adoration ought to be the first item on the worship agenda.

How can we worship in prayer? By first reflecting upon who God is and thanking Him for the things He has revealed about Himself. To worship in prayer is to allow our spirits to feast upon what God has revealed concerning His acts in the distant and recent past, and what He has told us about Himself. Slowly, as we review these things in a spirit of thanksgiving and recognition, we can sense our spirits beginning to expand, to take in the broader reality of God's presence and being. Slowly our consciousness is able to accept the fact that the universe about us is not closed or limited, but is in fact as expansive as the Creator meant for it to be. As we enter into worship we remind ourselves of how great He is.

Confession

In the light of God's majesty, we are called to an honesty about ourselves, what we are by contrast. This is the second aspect of prayer: confession. Spiritual discipline calls for a regular acknowledgement of our true nature and the specific acts and attitudes of the recent past that have not been pleasurable to God as He has sought our fellowship and our obedience.

"God be merciful to me a sinner" is an abbreviated version of the prayer of confession. We need the daily humbling experience of being broken before God as we face up to our imperfection, our propensity to seek evil ways. What has startled me as a Christian has been the constant awareness of new levels of sin that I had not spotted within myself before.

Some years ago, when Gail and I bought the old abandoned New Hampshire farm we now call Peace Ledge, we found the site where we wished to build our country home strewn with rocks and boulders. It was going to take a lot of hard work to clear it all out so there could be grass and plants. The whole family went to work on the clearing process. The first phase of the clearing project was easy. The big boulders went fast. And when they were gone, we began to see that there were a lot of smaller rocks that had to go too. And so we cleared the area again. But when we had cleared the site of the boulders and rocks, we noticed all of the stones and pebbles we had not seen before. This was much harder, more tedious work. But we stuck to it, and there came a day when the soil was ready for planting grass.

Our private lives are much like that field was. When I first began to follow Christ seriously, He pointed out many major behavior and attitude patterns that, like boulders, had to be removed. And as the years went by, many of those great big boulders did indeed get removed. But when they began to disappear, I discovered a whole new layer of action and attitude in my life that I had not previously seen. But Christ saw them and rebuked them one by one. The removal process began again. Then I reached that point in my Christian life at which Christ and I were dealing with stones and pebbles. They are too numerous to imagine, and as far as I can see, for the rest of my days on earth I will be working with the many stones and pebbles in my life. Every day at spiritual discipline time, there is likely to be a new stab at the clearing process.

But I must not leave this story without noting something else. Every spring at Peace Ledge, after the frost is out of the ground, we find that new stones and boulders appear around our country home. They have been beneath the surface of the ground, working their way up. And at their appointed times, one by one, they show up. Some of them are very frustrating to deal with because they look small until we try to remove them. And only then do we discover that there is more to those boulders than meets the eye.

My sinfulness is exactly the same. It consists of stones, pebbles, and boulders that come to the surface one by one. And the man or woman who ignores the daily experience of confession in spiritual discipline will soon be overwhelmed by them. I understand why the apostle Paul at an advanced age would call himself the "chief of sinners." Even while in jail facing the end of his life, he was still removing pebbles and boulders.

I smile at young believers who tell me that they are discouraged because of all the sin they see in their lives. The fact that they can at least see and feel repelled by that sin shows they are actually growing. There are too many people claiming to be followers of Christ who lost sight of their own sinfulness years ago. If they attend worship on Sunday, they leave without ever having had the experience of brokenness and repentance before God that indicates true worship. This leads to substandard Christianity.

E. Stanley Jones wrote of the importance of confession in our spiritual disciplines:

> I know that there are certain mental and emotional and moral and spiritual attitudes that are anti-health: anger, resentments, fear, worry, desire to dominate, self-preoccupation, guilts, sexual impurity, jealousy, a lack of creative activity, inferiorities, a lack of love.

These are the twelve apostles of ill health. *So in prayer I've learned to surrender these things to Jesus Christ as they appear.* I once asked Dr. Kagawa: "What is prayer?" And he answered: "Prayer is self-surrender." I agree. It is primarily self-surrender, blanket surrender, day by day. It is all we know and all we don't know. "All we don't know" covers the unfolding future and involves problems as they arise. So in prayer if any of these twelve things arise, and they do arise, for no one is free from the suggestion of anyone of them, I've learned how to deal with them: not to fight them, but to surrender them to Jesus Christ, and say, "Now, Lord, you have this."[7]

THE MINISTRY OF INTERCESSION

The great prayer warriors all seem to agree that intercession can begin only after we have fully worshiped. Having put ourselves in touch with the living God, we are prepared to pray with what Thomas Kelly called "the eyes of Heaven."

Old Commissioner Brengle was a man of prayer. His biographer wrote:

At prayer, he was a study in communion. It was his habit, except for those periods when he was too ill, to get out of bed between four and five o'clock in the morning and devote at least a full hour before breakfast to communion with his Lord. Dr. Hayes, whose book, *The Heights of Christian Devotion* carries these dedicatory words: "To Commissioner Samuel Logan Brengle, A Man of Prayer," gives us this glimpse:

"When Brengle has been a guest in my home, I often have found him on his knees with his open Bible on the bed or chair before him, reading his Bible through in that way and saying that the attitude helped him to turn all he read into personal petition:

'O Lord, help me to do this, or not to do that. Help me to be like this man, or to avoid this error.'"[8]

When worship has been completed, intercession can begin. Intercession usually means prayer on behalf of others. It is the greatest single ministry, in my opinion, that the Christian is privileged to have. And perhaps the most difficult.

Have you ever noticed that most faithful intercessors seem to be older people? Why? One reason may be that they have had to simplify their activities. But also note that older people may have become aware that intercession is much more effective than hours of unprayerful activity. And of course, experience through trial and error has taught them the wisdom of leaning on the reliable strength of God.

I have set out in the last few years to master the ministry of intercession for the sake of ministry to others. The progress is slow. Perhaps it is the greatest challenge of my private world.

The greater the spiritual authority and responsibility a person has, the more important it is that he develop intercessory capacities. That takes time and the sort of discipline many of us find difficult.

I think this is what the apostles, the leaders of the early congregation at Jerusalem, were getting at in Acts 6, when they asked for associates to take on the tasks of ministering to the widows and orphans so that they could "give [themselves] to prayer and to the preaching of the Word of God." Note what comes first on the priority list of these busy, busy men. They were starting to miss prayer and were quite nervous about the situation.

Intercession literally means to stand between two parties and plead the case of one to the other. Is there a greater example of intercession than the prayerful work of Moses, who gave himself to frequent strenuous petition on behalf of the wayward people of Israel?

For whom do we normally intercede? If married, for our spouses and children, obviously. But intercession also means widening the circle to take in close friends, those for whom God has made us responsible, the men and women with whom we work, and those in our congregations and neighborhoods whose personal needs are known to us.

My intercessory list includes many Christian leaders and organizations. There are many whom I know and like; but I must confess that I do not have much more than an occasional prayer burden for them. By contrast, there are some whose needs and pressures are very real to me, and I hold them before the Lord in my intercessory exercise every day. They find it of immense encouragement to hear me say, "I pray for you every day." Being responsible for a certain amount of Christian leadership myself, I have learned how supportive it feels to know that there is a handful of people who hold me before the throne of God in intercession every day.

Intercession means that we must take into account the mandate for world evangelization. In order to systematically pray around the world, I have divided up the continents in such a way that I can pray each day for one of them: Sunday, Latin America; Monday, Central America; Tuesday, North America; Wednesday, Europe; Thursday, Africa; Friday, Asia; and Saturday, the nations of the Pacific. In each area I include intercession for the national church, for missionaries with whom I am acquainted, and for the terrible suffering people are facing.

We are encouraged to bring our own petitions or requests before the Lord. Somehow I feel that these ought to come last in our prayer activity, but that is purely an opinion. I am thinking of matters in and about my personal life where it seems best to ask God for wisdom and supply. I have struggled with how much I should ask God for (some say everything) and how much He assumes we will handle ourselves. I don't know that I have a good answer to this. I discover as I grow in my faith that I am constrained to ask less and less for myself and more and more for others. And my personal requests tend to be more and more for resources and abilities that would be more of benefit for others.

The garden within our private world cannot remain uncultivated for long before it becomes infested with the sort of growth that makes it uninviting, both to the indwelling Lord and to us ourselves. When neglected for long, it becomes more like a dump than a garden. And then we have to rely upon external sources of strength and direction to keep moving ahead.

That was the reason for Howard Rutledge's struggle in the North Vietnam prison camp. By God's grace, he testifies, he made it through. But he never forgot what it is like to face such an ordeal when one's private world of the spirit has been left generally uncultivated.

A well-known Christian personality of the past century, Eric Liddell, the Olympic champion runner who was the hero of the movie *Chariots of Fire,* had a remarkably different experience in a prison in North China during World War II. His biographer speaks of the high esteem with which Liddell was held in the Weinsen Camp. And what was the secret of his extraordinary leadership power, his joy, and his integrity in the midst of enormous hardship? The biographer quotes a woman who was in the camp at the time and, with her husband, knew Liddell well:

> What was his secret? Once I asked him, but I really knew already, for my husband was in his dormitory and shared the secret with him. Every morning about 6 a.m., with curtains tightly drawn to keep in the

shining of our peanut-oil lamp, lest the prowling sentries would think someone was trying to escape, he used to climb out of his top bunk, past the sleeping forms of his dormitory mates. Then, at the small Chinese table, the two men would sit close together with the light just enough to illumine their Bibles and notebooks. Silently they read, prayed, thought about what should be done. *Eric was a man of prayer not only at set times* – though he did not like to miss a prayer meeting or communion service when such could be arranged. *He talked to God all the time, naturally, as one can who enters the "School of Prayer" to learn this way of inner discipline.* He seemed to have no weighty mental problems: his life was grounded in God, in faith, and in trust.[italics added][9]

To bring order to our private worlds is to cultivate the garden as Liddell did. From such exercises, according to the writer of Proverbs (4:23), comes a heart out of which flows life-giving energy.

At eighty years of age, bedridden with a stroke that impaired his speech and paralyzed his writing hand, E. Stanley Jones would ask himself: Can I handle this crisis? His answer: Absolutely. "The innermost strands are the strongest. I need no outer props to hold up my faith."

Sector Five

MEMO TO THE DISORGANIZED

If my private world is in order, it will be because I have chosen to press Sabbath peace into the rush and routine of my daily life in order to find the rest God prescribed for Himself and all of humanity.

FOURTEEN

Rest Beyond Leisure

WILLIAM WILBERFORCE, A COMMITTED CHRISTIAN, WAS a member of the English Parliament in the early years of the nineteenth century. As a politician he was noted for his vigorous leadership in convincing Parliament to pass a historic bill outlawing slavery in the British Empire. It was no mean feat. In fact, it may have been one of the greatest and most courageous acts of statesmanship in the history of democracy.

It took Wilberforce almost twenty years to construct the coalition of lawmakers that eventually passed the anti-slavery measure. It required detailed documentation of the injustices and cruelties of slavery, persuading lawmakers who did not want to offend the interests of big business, and standing strong against a host of political enemies who would have loved to see Wilberforce fall.

Wilberforce's spiritual strength and moral courage had to be immense. We learn something of the source of that strength and courage from an incident that occurred in 1801, some years before the anti-slavery measure was passed.

Lord Addington had led his party into power, and as the new prime minister he had begun to form a new cabinet. The central issue of the day in England was peace; Napoleon was terrorizing Europe, and the concern was whether or not England could stay out of war. Wilberforce was rumored to be among the candidates for a cabinet post, and because of the peace policy he found himself most anxious to gain the appointment. Garth Lean, one of Wilberforce's more recent biographers, told the story.

> It did not take long for Wilberforce to become preoccupied with the possibility of the appointment. For days it grabbed at his conscious mind, forcing aside everything else. By his own admission he had "risings of ambition," and it was crippling his soul.[1]

But there was a disciplined check and balance to Wilberforce's life, and in this particular situation that routine became indispensable. As Lean says, "Sunday brought the cure." For there came a regular time in Wilberforce's private world every week when he rested.

The Christian politician's journal tells the story best, in its entry at the end of that week of furious fantasizing and temptations to politic for position: "Blessed be to God for the day of rest and religious occupation wherein earthly things assume their true size. *Ambition is stunted*" (italics added).

Wilberforce's check and balance to a busy life was Sabbath; he had come to understand genuine rest. Wilberforce had discovered that the person who establishes a block of time for Sabbath rest on a regular basis is most likely to keep all of life in proper perspective and remain free of burnout and breakdown.

Not everyone in Wilberforce's public world held to that secret; workaholism and frantic busyness occurred in that day as it does today. About William Pitt, for example, Wilberforce wrote: "Poor fellow, he never schools his mind by a cessation from political ruminations, the most blinding, hardening and souring of all others." Of two other politicians who both took their own lives, Wilberforce wrote, "With peaceful

Sundays, the strings would never have snapped as they did from over-tension."

There can be little order in the private world of the human being when there is no appreciation for the meaning and pursuit of genuine rest, a cessation, as Wilberforce called it, in the routines of our times. From the beginning of all history, it has been an axiom at the base of healthy living; unfortunately, it is a principle badly misunderstood by those whose lives are driven to achievement and acquisition.

WE NEED REST

We are a tired people. Evidence of that fatigue abounds in a multitude of articles about health problems related to overwork and exhaustion. Stress management and stress relievers are terms that are commonly used in our vocabulary now. Workaholism is recognized as one of the great addictions. People who would never touch a drop of alcohol can be among the most serious work addicts.

And we excuse ourselves in our over work by telling one another that no matter how hard we are willing to work in our competitive world, there always seems to be someone willing to put in a few more hours than we are and take our job away.

What is strange about our general fatigue as a people is the fact that we are also such a leisure-oriented society. We are quite aware of the great leisure industry with its cruise ships, its fantasy resorts, and its tours to everywhere including Antarctica. The leisure industry is among the most profitable of all industries in our economy. Whole companies, organizations, and retail chain stores are committed to providing the clothing and equipment with which people can pursue fun and good times.

We probably have more time for leisure than we ever had before. The five-day workweek is, after all, a relatively new innovation in history; we have moved away from the farm, where there was always more work to do; we can leave work behind if we want and head for leisure. So why is there so much exhaustion and fatigue today? Is it real? Imagined? Or is the contemporary form of exhaustion evidence that we no longer understand genuine rest, which is different from the pursuit of leisure?

There is a biblical view of rest that needs to be uncovered and examined. In fact, the Bible reveals God Himself to be the first "rester": "On the seventh day, He rested" (Gen. 2:2). An even more enlightening comment is made by Moses in Exodus 31:17: "In six days the Lord made heaven and earth, but on the seventh day, He ceased from labour, and was refreshed." The literal translation suggests the phrase "He refreshed Himself."

Does God indeed need to rest? Of course not! But did God choose to rest? Yes. Why? Because God subjected creation to a rhythm of rest and work that He revealed by observing the rhythm Himself, as a precedent for everyone else. In this way, He showed us a key to order in our private worlds.

This rest was not meant to be a luxury, but rather a necessity for those who want to have growth and maturity. Since we have not understood that rest is a necessity, we have perverted its meaning, substituting for the rest that God first demonstrated things called leisure or amusement. These do not bring any order at all to the private world. Leisure and amusement may be enjoyable, but they are to the private world of the individual like cotton candy to the digestive system. They provide a momentary lift, but they will not last.

I am not by any means critical of the pursuit of fun-filled moments, diversion, laughter, or recreation. I am proposing that these alone will not restore the soul in the way that we crave. Although they may provide a sort of momentary rest for the body, they will not satisfy the deep need for rest within the private world.

Years ago there was a famous ad campaign for a liniment, which promised that the product would penetrate deeply into sore muscles, bringing relief from aches and pains. Sabbath rest penetrates to the deepest levels of fatigue in the inner, private world. This fatigue is rarely touched by any of the modern amusements.

THE MEANING OF SABBATH REST

Closing the Loop

When God rested, He looked upon His work, enjoyed its completed appearance, and then reflected upon its meaning: "And God saw that it was good" (Gen. 1:10). This shows us the first of the three principles of genuine rest. God gave His work meaning and acknowledged its completion. In so doing, He taught us that there is a necessary exercise of appreciation and dedication for our routines.

High-tech systems planners like to use the phrase "closing the loop" to describe the completion of a phase in an electrical circuit. They also use the phrase when they want to say that a task has been completed or that every person in a project has been informed or consulted.

So you could say that on the seventh day, God closed the loop on His primary creation activity. He closed it by resting and looking back upon it to survey what had been accomplished.

This rest then is, first of all, a time of looking backward, of loop-closing. We gaze upon our work and ask questions like: What does my work mean? For whom did I do this work? How well was the work done? Why did I do this? What results did I expect, and what did I receive?

To put it another way, the rest God instituted was meant first and foremost to cause us to interpret our work, to press meaning into it, to make sure we know to whom it is properly dedicated.

Brother Lawrence was a cook in a monastery. He learned to press meaning into virtually every action of his day. Note his capacity to see not only meaning but also purpose in his labour:

> I turn my little omelet in the pan for the love of God. When it is finished, if I have nothing to do, I prostrate myself on the ground and worship my God, who gave me this grace to make it, after which I arise happier than a king. When I can do nothing else, it is enough to have picked up a straw for the love of God. People look for ways of learning how to love God. They hope to attain it by I know not how many different practices. They take much trouble to abide in His presence by varied means. Is it not a shorter and more direct way to do everything for the love of God, to make use of all the tasks one's lot in life demands to show him that love, and to maintain his presence within by the communion of our heart with his? There is nothing complicated about it. One has only to turn to it honestly and simply.[2]

I am sure that most of us desire periods of time like that. The average worker has a desperate need to feel that his work means something, has significance, and is appreciated. But while we crave that assurance, we do not see the importance of taking time to gain it. A busyness, a frantic pace, sets in, and we delay our quest for meaning and interpretation; before long we have learned to get along without it. We lose sight of the question, What's this all for? We become content to allow the meaning and value of our work to be computed merely in the amount on our paychecks. Few people appreciate how dry and barren this leaves our private world.

A man I like very much was recently terminated by his company after twenty-two years of service. The economy had forced an across-the-board cutback, and his job was considered nonessential to the company's survival. He was out!

My friend was convinced that he would be hired by another company in the same field within a matter of days. After all, he told me, he had numerous connections, a profit-making record, and long-term service. He was not worried, he said. But several months passed with no offers. The "connections" dried up; no one responded to his feelers or to his résumés. He was reduced to sitting at home waiting for the phone to ring.

One day, after those many torturous months, he said to me, "This whole thing has forced me to do a lot of hard thinking. I've given myself to this career of mine for years, and look what it's gotten me. What was all this for anyway? Boy, have I gotten my eyes opened up."

Opened up to what? My friend is a fine Christian layman. But his eyes, by his own admission, had been closed to what his career had come to mean to him. What his eyes had opened up to was the fact that he had worked for years without asking what it all meant, what it was all for, and what might be the result. He had never discovered the exercise of reflection in the context of biblical rest.

A restless work style produces a restless person. Work that goes on month after month without a genuine pause to inquire of its meaning and purpose may swell the bank account and enhance the professional reputation. But it will drain the private world of vitality and joy. How important it is to regularly close loops on our activity.

Returning to the Eternal Truths

There is a second way biblical rest restores order to the private world. True rest is happening when we pause regularly amidst daily routines to sort out the truths and commitments by which we are living.

We are daily the objects of a bombardment of messages competing for our loyalties and labors. We are pushed and pulled in a thousand different directions, asked to make decisions and value judgments, to invest our resources and our time. By what standard of truth do we make these decisions?

God meant for His people to take a day each week in which this question was firmly dealt with. And in fact, He caused them to set aside a series of annual feast days during which major themes of eternal truth and divine action could be recalled and celebrated. You could call it a recalibration of the spirit.

Separating out the truths that are central to life is essential when one remembers that, according to Jeremiah, the heart is deceitful. We are vulnerable at all times to distortions of the truth, to persuasions that the true is really false and the false really true. Remember the words of the hymn writer:

> Prone to wonder, Lord, I feel it;
> Prone to leave the God I love.

(Robert Robinson)

The hymn reflects upon the inexorable inward drift that must be regularly checked by measuring our thoughts and values against the eternal truths that have been revealed through the Scripture and the mighty acts of God.

The Jewish theologian Abraham Joshua Heschel looked at rest in the Sabbath tradition and wrote:

> The meaning of the Sabbath is to celebrate time rather than space. Six days a week, we live under the tyranny of things of space; on the Sabbath we try to become attuned to holiness in time. It is a day on which we are called upon to share what is eternal in time, to turn from the results of creation to the mystery of creation; from the world of creation to the creation of the world.[3]

We need to ask ourselves, Is this happening in my own private world?

The clapboards of our New Hampshire home expand and contract in response to temperature extremes. The result is that some nails work loose and have to be pounded back in to regain a snug hold. This "repounding" is what happens during a genuine rest period, be it in the privacy of that quiet day or in the midst of a congregation while we worship the living God.

One of the great joys of repeating the traditional creeds of the Christian church is that it gives us an opportunity to reaffirm the central truths of God's revelation. As we say, "I believe . . ." we begin to hammer back the nails of our convictions and commitments. And we separate those beliefs out from what we choose not to believe.

The same thing happens when we sing grand old hymns and pray certain prayers. The nails are being pounded back in, and order is being restored to a drifting spirit in our private worlds. Reaffirmations occur on that special rest day, if we take time in private for reading, meditating, and reflecting.

My wife shares with me an entry in her journal on this very subject:

A glorious Lord's Day. Have been reading at length about the Sabbath. Feel more and more strongly that I've not fully utilized God's command to rest.

It's not a rule that restricts but it is a rule that liberates. For He made me to need rest. And physically and mentally we are freed to better performance if we live within His "design specifications." And it is a day of reminding us who God is. Every seventh day I need to come back to the fixed Centre.

Don Stephenson remarked today that for him and others Sunday is just that – a day to come back to the straight edge and be encouraged to go back to the "mire."

I would propose that we need to ask hard questions, both of ourselves and of our churches, concerning whether or not the sort of rest that reaffirms truth is actually happening. It is possible for Christians and their churches to become so busy carrying on programs – for whatever good purpose – that the worship-rest necessary to the private world never happens.

Thus, rest is not only a looking back at the meaning of my work and the path I have so recently walked in my life; but is also a refreshing of my belief and commitment to Christ. It is a fine tuning of my inner navigational instruments so that I can make my way through the world for another week.

Defining Our Mission

If the first two meanings centered on what was past and present, this one centers on the future. When we rest in the biblical sense, we affirm our intentions to pursue a Christ-centered tomorrow. We ponder where we are headed in the coming week, month, or year. We define our intentions and make our dedications.

General George Patton demanded that his men know and be able to articulate exactly what the current mission was. "What is your mission?" he would frequently ask. The definition of the mission was the most important piece of information a soldier could carry into combat. Based on that knowledge, he could make his decisions and implement the plan. That is exactly what happens when I pursue biblical rest. I take a hard look at my mission. And it has taught me to make a small pause even in my spiritual disciplines each morning to ask the question, What is my mission today? Not to regularly ask this question is to leave yourself open to mistakes of judgment and direction.

Jesus often withdrew to seek solitude. While others were lulled to the rest of sleep, Jesus was drawn to the rest of gaining strength and direction for His next phase of mission. No wonder He met every encounter with a fresh burst of wisdom. No wonder He had ample courage not to fight back, not to defend Himself. His spirit was always rested, His private world ordered. Without this kind of rest our private world will always be strained and disordered.

CHOOSING TO REST

One of the noted vicars of the Church of England was Charles Simeon, of Holy Trinity Church in Cambridge. For more than fifty years he preached from its pulpit, and the people crowded the sanctuary, standing in the aisles to hear him.

Simeon was a fellow at Kings College, and he lived in apartments that overlooked the courtyard in the college complex. His second-floor dwellings provided him an exclusive opening out to the roof where he would often walk, one of his physical forms of rest, while he talked with God. That rooftop became known as Simeon's walk.

A busy and brilliant man, Simeon was in touch with students at the colleges in Cambridge, with a large congregation, and with church and missionary leaders around the world. He wrote (in longhand) literally thousands of letters, edited fifty books of his own sermons, and served as one of the founders of several major missionary organizations. But he never ceased to find time for the rest that his private world demanded.

A sample of his private exercises can be found in this entry to his journal, recorded by Hugh Hopkins, a Simeon biographer.

> I spent this day as I have for these 43 last years, as a day of humiliation; having increased need of such season every year I live.

Hopkins wrote:

> Self-humiliation for Charles Simeon consisted not of belittling the gifts that God had given him or pretending that he was a man of no account, or exaggerating the sins of which he was very conscious. He went about it by consciously bringing himself into the presence of God, dwelling thoughtfully on his majesty and glory, magnifying the mercy of his forgiveness and the wonder of his love. These were the things that humbled him – not so much his own sinfulness but God's incredible love.[4]

Simeon enjoyed a lifelong effectiveness under enormous strain. I have no doubt that a large part of his secret of endurance was his deliberate and disciplined pursuit of Sabbath rest.

For the Jew, the Sabbath was first of all a day. A day set aside in obedience to God. The law forbade work of any kind, allowing only the sort of observances such as we have already reviewed. Christians have little idea of how special the Sabbath was to pious Jews. We would do well to listen and hear what they think. An Israeli tourist brochure tells us that one rabbi wrote of Sabbath:

> Make the Sabbath an eternal monument of the knowledge and sanctification of God, both in the centre of your busy public life and in the peaceful retreat of your domestic hearth. For six days cultivate the earth and rule it . . . But the seventh is the Sabbath of the Lord thy God . . . Let [a man] therefore realize that the Creator of old is the living God of today, [that He] watches every man and every human effort, to see how man uses or abuses the world loaned to him and the forces bestowed upon him, and that He is the sole architect to Whom every man has to render an account of his week's labours.

What is important behind these statements is the Jewish awareness of a unique pace to Sabbath. Routines are to stop; labour is to cease. Even the homemaker in the pious Jewish family is to refrain from cooking or menial tasks. Food is prepared before Sabbath begins so that she also can enjoy the fruit of the special rest day. This is a far cry from the incredible, filled-up, pressurized day many evangelical Christians tend to make of their "day of rest."

Sabbath is first of all a day. In our Christian tradition we have chosen to make that day not the seventh, as the Jew does, but the first day of the week, in recognition of the resurrection of Christ. But having made that choice, what have we done with our day – this time that God gave as a special gift?

A man with whom I worship every week said to me after one particularly long Sunday of church activity, "I'm sure glad that there is only one rest day per week. I'd burn out if we had to go through two 'days of rest' like this every seven days."

His humour conveys a serious charge against many Christian leaders and churches who have turned Sunday into a day of unrest, perhaps for some the most tension-filled day of the week.

But Sabbath is more than just a day. It is a principle of rest along the lines of the three dimensions I have already mentioned. And what might happen should we choose the peace of Sabbath rest rather than the fun of secular leisure?

First, Sabbath rest means worship with the Christian family. In proper worship we will have a chance to exercise all three aspects that lead to the rest of our private worlds: looking backward, upward, and ahead. Such worship is non-negotiable to the person committed to walking with God.

I am moved by the words of Luke who described the Sabbath discipline of Jesus: "And He came to Nazareth, where He had been brought up; and as was His custom, He entered the synagogue on the Sabbath" (Luke 4:16, italics added). One never sees Christ slipping away from the public worship of the Father.

But second, Sabbath means a deliberate acceptance of personal rest and tranquillity within the individual life. Sabbath means a rest that brings peace into the private world. As Christ pressed stillness into a storm, order into the being of a demon-possessed maniac, health into a desperately sick woman, and life into a dead friend, so He seeks to press peace into the harried private world of the man or woman who has been in the marketplace all week. But there is a condition. We must accept this peace as a gift and take the time to receive it.

As a pastor, I have long felt that Sunday was anything but Sabbath rest for my wife and me. It was many years into my Christian adulthood before I realized that I had been robbing myself of a necessary form of restoration. The fact was that I needed some sort of Sabbath for my own private world, and I wasn't getting it. When I looked at my Sundays, it seemed impossible to think that I would ever enjoy Sabbath's rejuvenating gift. How could I preach three Sunday morning sermons and a frequent evening sermon, as well as be available throughout the day to the people of my congregation, and expect to be restored? Rarely did a Sunday end without Gail and me being on the verge of exhaustion. Day of rest indeed!

What to do? A few years ago, the Grace Chapel congregation was gracious enough to give me a four-month sabbatical leave. Rather than go off to a university to study, I chose to go to New Hampshire, where we built Peace Ledge. The outstanding experience of those four months was the silence and peace we discovered on Sundays.

Although I enjoyed the construction of Peace Ledge immensely, I promised myself that I would do no work on the Lord's Day. Thus, when Sunday came, we spent a few early morning hours reading, thinking, and praying. And then we went to a local church where we could worship. We did not know many of the people, but we tried to throw ourselves into the worship and draw from the prayers, the hymns, and the sermon food for our spirits. We made it a time of affirming our convictions, thanking God for blessings, and committing ourselves to the coming week in which we would try to reflect the honour of the Lord.

Our Sunday afternoons during the four months were quiet hours for walks in the woods, deep conversation, and a searching process as we evaluated our spiritual disciplines and Christian progress. It was a marvellously restful Sabbath experience for us; I had never known what it could be like before that time.

We were hooked on Sabbaths when we returned from our sabbatical. But suddenly it was back to sermons, and counselling, and programming. Business as usual on Sunday. We felt robbed! And so it was that we decided *our* Sabbath would be another day of the week. We were not going to miss God's gift! On Sundays, we would try to help others enjoy their Sabbaths. But for us the peace normally reserved for that day would have to happen at some other time. And that was fine.

Sabbath for Gail and me became Thursday. To the extent that we could achieve it, we budgeted that day of the week for rest in our private worlds. It meant total withdrawal from our congregation whenever possible, even laying aside the routines of our home if we could. We learned that if we were going to be useful to those associated with us in ministry, to our children, and to the congregation, we would have to jealously guard this opportunity for spiritual restoration.

There is no legalism here – rather a freedom to accept a gift. Frankly, I think some have destroyed the joy of Sabbath, as did the Pharisees, by surrounding it with prescriptive laws and precedents. That is not our Sabbath. Our Sabbath was made for us, given to us by God. Its purpose is worship and restoration, and whatever it takes to make that happen, we will do.

It is important to say that we probably could not have pursued Sabbath rest as easily when our children were young and needed more constant attention. And it is also important to say, as Gail often observes, that we do our people a favour by withdrawing from them for rest. For when we return, we have something to offer that God probably could not have given us in any other atmosphere.

Obviously, every Thursday could not be budgeted for Sabbath. But we discovered that if we made a regular attempt at such a discipline, the results were tremendous. Our private worlds were indeed substantially reordered. The most astounding discovery was that I felt not only rested but able to use the times of other days in a far more effective fashion.

What had happened, much to my amazement, was that by bringing this restful order to my private world through proper Sabbath observance, I was able to impact my public world in the days that followed with much greater wisdom and judgement.

I believe that Sabbath rest may mean a day a week. But it can happen at any time, in large and small doses, when we choose to set aside an hour or more for the pursuit of intimacy with God. All of us need a "Simeon's walk."

But let me be quick to underscore that this rest, which is sabbathlike, ought to be a fixed allocation in the budgeting of our time. We do not rest because our work is done; we rest because God commanded it and created us to have a need for it.

That is important to think about, because our current view of rest and leisure denies that principle. Most of us think of resting as something we do *after* our work is done. But Sabbath is not something that happens after. It may in fact be something that is pursued *before*. If we assume that this rest comes only after work is complete, many of us are in trouble, for we have jobs where the work is never finished. And that in part is why some of us rarely rest; never finishing our work, no time for Sabbath peace and restoration.

I had to learn to pursue Sabbath rest without a sense of guilt. I had to realize that there was nothing wrong with laying aside other work for the purpose of enjoying God's gift of special time. Thus, Sabbaths have gone into our calendars with regularity. They are planned weeks in advance, along with other priorities. And when someone has proposed a supper, a ball game, or a committee meeting on a day set aside for the reordering of our private worlds, my wife and I have simply said, "Sorry, we have a commitment on that day. It's Sabbath for us."

It was this sort of discipline that enabled William Wilberforce to overcome the consuming thrust of ambition that had crippled his private world for so many days. Having reached the day of rest, he slipped back into that centre where God was in full control. He saw things in their true size. "Ambition is stunted," he wrote.

One wonders what would have happened if Wilberforce had not had that Sabbath check and balance to face his ambitious nature. Would he have been deterred from his call to lead England away from slavery? Probably. You have to believe that in taking Sabbath, he was able to detect a deviation from his original sense of purpose and, just in time, regain the right course. Because he got back on track, the great landmark achievement of abolition was his to claim.

The world and the church need genuinely *rested* Christians: Christians who are regularly refreshed by true Sabbath rest, not just leisure or time off. When a godly rest is achieved, you will see just how tough and resilient Christians can actually be.

MEMO TO THE DISORGANIZED

If my private world is in order, it will be because I have made a deliberate decision to begin the "ordering" process. Now!

EPILOGUE

The Spinning Wheel

ONE OF THE CELEBRATED HEROES OF THE 20TH CENTURY has been Mohandas Gandhi, the Indian leader who sparked the flame of independence for his country. Those who have read his biographies or who have seen his story so brilliantly told upon the screen are often impressed with the tranquil spirit that "India's George Washington" displayed.

Serenity? We see Gandhi among the most poverty-ridden people of Indian cities, where death and disease are rampant. He touches them, offers a word of hope, provides a gentle smile. But a day later the same man is found in palaces and government buildings, where he negotiates with the most clever men of his age. And the question arises: How did he manage to span the gap between the two extremes of people and circumstances?

How could Gandhi maintain his private sense of order, his appropriate humility, and his base wisdom and judgement? How did he avoid losing his own identity and spirit of conviction as he moved between those enormous extremes? Where did the emotional and spiritual force come from?

Perhaps the beginning of an answer to those questions lies in Gandhi's fascination with the simple spinning wheel. The wheel seems to have always been at the centre of his life. Gandhi appears to have often returned from public exposure to his humble dwellings where he would, in Indian fashion, sit upon the floor and engage in the simple act of spinning the wool from which his clothes were made.

What was he trying to do? Was this merely part of a plan to project a certain image? Was it purely a political attempt to identify with the masses, whose loyalty he held in his grasp? Perhaps it was even a statement to all Indians. Maybe Gandhi was saying, "Stop buying the finished textile products of England and contributing to its wealth when you could be contributing to the welfare of India." I would suggest that it was much, much more. But I have even another idea.

I think Gandhi's spinning wheel was his centre of gravity in life. It was the great leveller in his human experience. When he returned from the great public moments in his life, the spinning-wheel experience restored him to his proper sense of proportion, so that he was not falsely swelled with pride due to the cheers of the people. When he withdrew from the moments of encounter with kings and government leaders, he was not tempted to think of himself in some inflated fashion when he moved to the work of the wheel.

The spinning wheel was always a reminder to Gandhi of who he was and what the practical things in life were all about. In engaging in this regular exercise, he was resisting all the forces of his public world that tried to distort who he knew himself to be.

Gandhi was by no means a Christian, but what he was doing at the wheel is an indispensable lesson for any healthy Christian. For he shows us what every man or woman who wants to move in a public world without being pressed into its mould needs to do. We, too, need the spinning-wheel experience – the ordering of our private worlds so that they are constantly restructured in strength and vitality.

Not long ago I met a very distinguished older man who had been the president of a small, well-known college in the eastern United States. He was deeply admired by all who knew him. In getting acquainted, I learned that, during the years of his college presidency, he had maintained the habit of disappearing from campus life perhaps as many times as twice a year. To do what? To take a job for a couple of weeks where he would familiarize himself with the experiences of people who did not enjoy the vocational privileges he had. So he would become a garbage collector, or a shoe-shine man, or a busboy in a restaurant. What he said to me about it all was, "I always wanted to make sure that I understood the life of those who weren't as insulated from the real world as I was as a college president."

As Thomas Kelly says, "We are trying to be several selves at once, without all our selves being organized by a single, mastering Life within us." Again he says, "Life is meant to be lived from a Centre, a divine Centre. Each one of us can live such a life of amazing power and peace and serenity, of integration and confidence and simplified multiplicity, on one condition – that is, if we really want to."

And that is the condition with which we must finally deal. Do we really want order within our private worlds? Again, do we want it?

If it is true that actions speak louder than words, it would appear that the average Christian does not really seek an ordered private world as a top priority. It would seem that we prefer to find our human effectiveness through busyness, frantic programming, material accumulation, and rushing to various conferences, seminars, film series, and special speakers.

In short, we try to bring order to the inner world by beginning with activity in the outer one. This is exactly the opposite of what the Bible teaches us, what the great saints have shown us, and what our dismal spiritual experiences regularly prove to us.

Somewhere John Wesley is quoted as saying of life in his public world, "Though I am always in haste, I am never in a hurry, because I never undertake more work than I can go through with calmness of spirit."

I once enjoyed a close working relationship with a man who was a stargazer. Regularly he would spend an evening in the countryside, where he could turn his telescope on the darkened sky. But he had to leave the city in order to escape all the light that pollutes the atmosphere. Once he'd left the light behind, the picture of the sky became much clearer.

How do we escape such interference in order to gaze into the inner space of our private world? That question remains dangerously unanswered in too many lives. Men and women who command the leadership of large organizations and churches too often are unable to answer the question for themselves. Simple people, busy earning a living and trying to keep up with the Joneses, are wrestling with the question. It yields no easy answer – only a simple one. We escape into the space of the inner world only when we determine that it is an activity more important than anything else we do.

Although I have always believed in the priority of ordering my inner world, it has only begun to become a reality for me as I have moved into the older years of my life. And now that I have grown increasingly aware of my limits, my weaknesses, and even the approach of that time when my own life shall end, I find it more possible to look within and cultivate the spinning-wheel experience so that inner strength and spiritual vitality can become a resource.

It is at that centre that we begin to see Jesus Christ in all His majesty. There He is more than what is contained in some doctrinal statement about Him. He is more than the mushy words of some contemporary songs. At the centre, He commands attention as the risen Lord of life; and we are compelled to follow after Him and draw from the strength of His character and compassion.

At the centre, we are appropriately awed by the splendour and majesty of God as heavenly Father. There is solemn but joyful worship; there are confession and breaking. And there is forgiveness, restoration, and assurance.

Finally, at the centre, we are filled by the power and strength of God as Holy Spirit. There is a resurgence of confidence and expectancy. We receive insight and wisdom; faith that removes mountains is generated, and a love for others, even for the unlovable, begins to grow.

When we come from an experience at the spinning wheel, where all is returned to proper proportion and value, the public world can be managed and properly touched. Relationships with family and friends, with business associates, neighbours, and even enemies take on a new and healthier perspective. It becomes possible to forgive, to serve, to not seek vengeance, to be generous.

Our work will be affected by exercise at the centre. Work will be given new meaning and a higher standard of excellence. Integrity and honesty will become important items of pursuit. Fear will be lost, and compassion will be gained.

Coming from the spinning-wheel experience, we are less apt to be seduced by the false promises and seductions of those out to capture the soul.

All of this and much more goes into motion when the private world is ordered first – before the Christian walks in the public world.

Not to do that is to invite the sinkhole syndrome. And history abounds with examples of people who own that consequence.

Today our public worlds demand a few good people who can walk among the masses and negotiate with the powerful, but never change, never capitulate, never compromise.

And how will they manage that? By pursuing the spinning-wheel experience: the retreat into the silent centre where time can be ordered by priorities, where the mind can be tuned to discover God's creation, the spirit can be sharpened, and where there is the quietness of Sabbath rest. This is the private world, and when given proper attention, it comes to order.

Study Guide

BY LESLIE H. STOBBLE

Working through a study guide about ordering our private worlds may seem a peculiarly activistic response to a call for more inner-directed living. Yet most of us need something to help us develop a more disciplined approach to ordering our private worlds as believers.

The author reflects, "I found that one practical way to learn to listen to God speak in the garden of my private world was to keep a journal. With pencil in hand ready to write, I found that there was an expectancy, a readiness to hear anything God might wish to whisper through my reading and reflection." (p. 175).

We hope this study guide will aid the reader in establishing a reflective writing as a habit. Some questions are designed to get you to think through the implications of the author's suggestions and to write down your responses. Others we hope will trigger life responses.

* Questions with an asterisk have been inserted to facilitate discussion in group settings.

–> *Readers who do not wish to write in their book may download a copy of this study for printing on a PC printer* for their own use: www.highlandbks.com *and go to page 'downloads'.*

STUDY GUIDE

Preface

1. What experience or insight triggered your desire to read *Ordering Your Private World*?

2. What enemy (or enemies) of order to your private world do you need to identify?

3. Who is your most persistent advocate of ordering your private world? Compare Ephesians 1:13 with John 14:26.

4. List the five sectors of your private world that need ordering. See p. 39.

a.

b.

c.

d.

e.

Now rate yourself on a scale of 1-10 for each
category, with ten representing perfection.

* 5.   What biographies have motivated you to move
       toward a more ordered inner life? What made these
       persons so influential?

Chapter One: The Sinkhole Syndrome

1.   In what ways has your life during the past year
       illustrated the author's words: "Our outer, or
       public, world is easier to deal with. It is much more
       measurable, visible, and expandable"?

* 2.   What might be described as a "sinkhole experience"
       in your life?

3.   The author writes that the private world "is a centre
       in which choices and values can be determined,
       where solitude and reflection might be pursued."
       What else can happen there as well, according to
       the author? See page 22.

* 4. Which public worlds are screaming for your attention? Put an asterisk beside the ones to which you've capitulated.

5. What are some fears that may have prevented your seeking the inner peace that steals over a well-ordered inner world?

* 6. Looking ahead, can you think of an event or pressure that could become powerful enough to become a sinkhole in your life?

* 7. Read Ephesians 3:14-21. What connection do you see between verse 20 and verse 16?

Chapter Two: A View from the Bridge

1. Read the story of the submarine captain on pages 31 and 32. Now compare this with the "bridge" appearance described in Acts 27:21-25. What can we learn from the apostle Paul's expression of confidence?

2. If you were a Christian counsellor and a Jerald H. Maxwell (see page 33) came to you, what would you tell him, based on Jesus' response to the disciples in the storm on the Sea of Galilee?

* 3. Where do we need to build up resources to be able to withstand the steadily mounting pressures of the world around us? See Romans 12:2.

4.   What set Mary Slessor apart from others of her generation? See page 37.

* 5. From your circle of friends and people you have read about, who would be your best contemporary model of inner orderliness? Why?

* 6. What are the two most important choices you can make to gain this kind of inner "bridge"? See page 36.

a.

b.

Chapter Three: Caught in a Golden Cage

1. Christ separated people out on the basis of their
    tendency to be driven or their willingness to be
    called. He dealt with their motives, the basis of their
    spiritual energy, and the sorts of gratification in
    which they were interested. He called those who
    were drawn to Him and avoided those who were
    driven and wanted to use Him. Assuming this to be
    true, would you have qualified as one of Jesus'
    disciples? If not qualified, why not?

2. Make an attempt to sort out and catalogue the
    motives that energize you as an involved Christian.
    Take time to listen to the quiet voice of the Holy
    Spirit and begin to write.

3. What are some of the negative components of stress
    in your life today?

* 4. List the stresses the apostle Paul experienced in his life of ministry as described in 2 Corinthians 11:24-28. Reflect upon them by comparing them with the negative components of stress that you listed for the preceding questions.

5. How did Paul gain the inner resilience needed for his stress level? Using a concordance, isolate the words pray and prayer in the apostle's letter for the inner ordering of his world.

6. List the characteristics of the driven person that are obvious in your life from your perspective.

7. Now ask your spouse or your closest friend to pinpoint those characteristics in your life.

* 8. With what three assets had God blessed Saul at the time he became king? (see pages 56-59) What advantage did they gain him?

a.

b.

c.

9. As your read the account of Saul's experience, write down the parallels in your own life.

10. Now lay these before the Lord, asking Him for insight into action you can take to get out of the golden cage. List action points below as they come to you.

* 11. How can we help Christian leaders trapped by the golden-cage syndrome?

Chapter Four: The Tragic Tale of a Successful Bum

1. Reflecting on the story of the driven husband that opens the chapter, examine experiences during your formative years that may have shaped your present attitudes. Describe each with a one-sentence statement that pinpoints the key issue. If they were positive, take time to thank God for each one.

* 2. Make a two-column chart. In the first column list the external goals of the driven man (see p. 64) and in the second column the parallels you recognize in your life.

* 3. List the motivational basis for people you know who may be driven, drawing on the reasons given on pages 64-68.

4. Which of these motivational mainsprings shape your inner world? Describe how they affect your actions.

5. What experiences does the author consider critical to changing the lifestyle of the driven person? See page 68.

* 6. Identify the key elements in Peter's interaction with Jesus that produced change. Consider Matthew 14:25-30, 16:13-17, 26:31-35, and John 21:15-22, among others.

7. Whom do you need to forgive for the drivenness in your life? What action will you take to gain the release that forgiveness can give you both?

* 8. Do all of us have to experience a classic confrontation with Jesus as Paul did before we can change from being driven persons to called persons? If so, why? If not, why not?

Chapter Five: Living as a Called Person

1. According to the author, what is the difference between a driven person and a called person? See page 72. What category do you seem to fit?

* 2. How do the disciples of Jesus match the apostle Paul's description of the called in 1 Corinthians 1:26-31?

3. When do we see the difference between John the Baptist and King Saul most vividly? See page 74.

* 4. What are the characteristics of the called person, according to the author? See pages 75-80.

5. If you were to measure yourself according to those characteristics, what is your weakest link? Set aside a specific time to be before the Lord and let the Holy Spirit do His gracious work in you. Either make a journal entry or record your experience here.

6. What do you sense is your primary purpose as a Christian servant?

7.   Write out your "desert" experience. If you cannot identify one, plan for a specific time when you can be alone with God and settle your purpose and priorities. Then write them out.

* 8.   Describe two or more life situations in which the lessons John learned in the desert would help you in today's environment.

9.   The author asks, "What makes you tick Why are you doing all of that? What do you hope to gain as a result? And what would be your reaction if it was all taken away?" (p. 87). Write out your answers after you have had time to reflect on the questions.

Chapter Six: Has Anyone Seen My Time? I've Misplaced It!

1.   How do you respond to each of the following statements?

a. My desk has a cluttered appearance.

b. I am aware of a diminution in my self-esteem.

c. There are a series of forgotten appointments,
    telephone messages to which I have failed to
    respond, and deadlines I have begun to miss.

d. I tend to invest my energies in unproductive tasks.

e. I do not feel good about the quality of my work.

f.   I do not experience intimacy with God on a regular basis.

g.   My personal relationships are suffering.

h.   I really don't like myself, my job, or much of anything else.

2.   None of us can effect improvement in that many areas at once. We need about three weeks to break a habit and another three to feel comfortable with a new once. So set your sight on changing the area that you consider most critical at this time in your ordering of your private world. Then mark on your calendar when you will focus on the second area. Below, note the two areas you have selected for improvement.

a.

b.

* 3.   In beginning to budget time effectively, you must
       establish priorities within the framework of your life
       calling. How does Jesus illustrate this in Luke 18 as
       He sets out for Jerusalem?

4.   What do you consider your number one mission in
       life? In what way does it (should it) inform your
       time schedule?

5.   Jesus understood His limits, says the author. In what
       ways could you be exceeding the natural limits God
       has given you for your life?

* 6. Moses had forty years in the wilderness; David, his years of exile from the court of Saul; Jesus, thirty years to begin His ministry. Describe what you could consider a similar, usually unexplainable delay in getting on with your mission in life. Can you list discernible benefits from that time?

7. Jesus invested His life in twelve disciples. In whom are you investing your life as a parent, as a businessperson, as a leader in your church, as a professional? What are you trying to achieve in your discipling role?

* 8. What can you do to multiply your ministry as Jesus did?

Chapter Seven: Recapturing My Time

1. Complete the following sentence: I am least
    effective in managing my time in my (describe
    sphere of activity)...

* 2. Check the validity of MacDonald's four laws of
    unseized time based on your experiences. Copy
    each law and then describe one situation where that
    law has been in operation in you life.

a.

b.

c.

d.

3. If you are in a group, share some of these.

    List two of your tasks that you could pass on to your
    spouse, associate, lay leader (if you are a pastor),
    secretary, son, or daughter without detracting from
    what you do best. (This may be a task you really
    enjoy doing, but one you know is not central to
    your life mission.)

a.

b.

4. Suggest why the "strong people" in your life rob you of valuable time you could give to your family.

5. What are you doing for the sake of public acclaim? You may need to work out this answer before the Lord in a special time with Him.

6. What would happen if you were to implement John 9:4 in your life?

7.   Is there anything in your life about which you feel
     as strongly as Jesus did about going to Jerusalem, as
     recorded in Matthew 16:21?

8.   Analyze your life rhythms. When are you most
     effective? What can you do to match your most
     effective moments with your most significant tasks?

* 9. List the criteria you can use to distinguish the good
      from the best for you in light of your
      responsibilities.

10. What portions of your day/week should you be
     budgeting far in advance so you can fend off
     intruders?

* 11. What were Jesus' time priorities according to these passages: Luke 4:16; 4:42-43; 5:27; 6:12; 9:21-22; 18:16; 19:5?

Chapter Eight: The Better Man Lost

* 1. What is the greatest danger of flabby thinking (see p. 123) in a church or in a society? If there is a specific example in your life, describe the situation.

2. Describe a situation in which you were mentally ready for the challenge because you had developed mental toughness.

* 3. What request by the apostle Paul indicates he was determined to stay mentally tough even while in prison? See 2 Timothy 4:13.

4. What could be considered danger signals that indicate you are a fast starter, a personal quality you have considered a positive benefit until now?

5. What provides you with the mental stimulation you know you should be getting, but you have not given it priority?

a. Specific reading to enlarge your base of information.

b. Professional seminars that enrich and challenge your thinking.

c. A mentor or close friend who consistently challenges your thinking.

d. Other.

6. What percentage of your reading or your interaction with others challenges your status quo? Name two books you have read with which you disagreed.

* 7. List some of the indicators of mental toughness in Paul's address to the Athenians in Acts 17:16-32.

8. The author writes, "The best kind of thinking is accomplished when it is done in the context of reverence for God's kingly reign over all creation." What kind of preparation will you need to do to develop that context?

9. A Presbyterian pastor annually speaks and fields questions at a local "skeptics corner" attended only by unbelievers. This heavy interaction with the non-Christian mind sharpens his awareness of the enemy's tactics. What can you do to achieve a similar result?

* 10. What are some of the non-Christian ideas we can fall prey to when our minds become dull?

11. What are some areas of your thought life that need
     expanding and toughening? Beside each area, list a
     resource that you can tap to help you.

Chapter Nine: The Sadness of a Book Never Read

* 1. The author suggests we need to learn to think
      Christianly. What does that mean? See page 140.

2. If you do not have the advantage of growing up in a
    strongly Christian environment, what can you do to
    "catch up"?

3. In what parts of your world can you learn to
    "appreciate the messages God has written in
    creation"?

* 4. What can you do to enhance your storehouse of
information, ideas, and insights?

5. List the four steps in becoming a listener. Then
describe what you can do to personalize these steps
in your listening process.

a.

b.

c.

d.

6. Describe a situation in which listening to God or to
another person helped you take a major step
forward.

7. What book have you wanted to read for a long time and just never got to? When can you get it into your schedule?

8. What set Ezra apart from other leaders of his day? Turn to Psalm 119:33-40 and describe the characteristics of this kind of student.

* 9. What are your obstacles to beginning a program of offensive study if you do not already have one?

* 10. What areas should we as Christians study intensively if we are to make a significant difference in our world?

11. What area of offensive study do you need to begin if you are to achieve excellence as a servant in your position? List the top resource that you need to acquire to do so.

Chapter Ten: Order in the Garden

1. If you were confined to a prisoner-of-war camp without a Bible, how effective would you be in recalling Scripture? What can you do to learn more Scripture?

2. If you were totally honest with yourself, how would you describe your inner communion with God?

* 3. The author writes, "If we are ever to develop a spiritual life that gives contentment, it will be because we approach spiritual living as a discipline, much as the athlete trains his body for competition." Do you agree or disagree? If you disagree, write out your reasons.

* 4. What are some of the metaphors you would use to describe your inner spiritual centre?

5. Write out the five privileges we lose if we do not have a disciplined approach to inner spiritual development (see pages 162 - 164). Now check off those you sense are missing in your life.

a.

b.

c.

d.

e.

6.   What pressure situations in life helped you begin the development of your inner spiritual life?

7.   What is the deepest desire of your heart for your inner life with God? What can you do to have that desire satisfied?

* 8.   What did David gain from his communion with God, as described in Psalm 27?

Chapter Eleven: No Outer Props Necessary

1.   If you were to be left helpless by a physical disability, where would you turn for the strength to survive?

2. What was the secret of E. Stanley Jones's serenity
    when he was disabled by a stroke?

3. Write out the four spiritual exercises recommended
    as critical (see p. 170) and give yourself a rating
    from 1 to 10 on each (with 10 as the best).

a.

b.

c.

d.

4. Describe some of the noisy intrusions in your life
    that rob you of the silence and solitude the author
    recommends.

* 5. What can we learn from the silence/solitude of Zacharias; his wife, Elizabeth; and Mary, the mother of Jesus?

6. The author describes the difficulties in quieting the inner self to attain solitude. Try it and write down the results.

* 7. What aids do you employ to listen to God in your private world?

8. What is the key contribution of a personal journal?

9. What are some of the things the author records in his journal? See page 178-182.

10. Use this space to make your first journal entry if you have not yet started journaling. Let it be your experiment.

Chapter Twelve: Everything Has to Be Entered

1. Describe a time in your life when neither the inner strands nor the outer props were strong enough to hold you up. If you have not had such an experience, describe how you avoided such a time.

2. Describe an experience you or someone you know has had that is similar to that of Samuel in the Old Testament (see page 189).

3. What does the author call the "enter" key for effective internalization of what we hear in silence and solitude?

4. What happens in meditation, according to the author? See page 190.

5. Stop to meditate on your favourite psalm. If you do not have one, take time with Psalm 139.

6. The author writes, "We often enter the chamber to meet with God while we are still emotionally out of breath." If this has happened to you, what can you do to prevent it in the future?

* 7. List the two great Christian classics that you want to read during the next six months.

* 8. How can you use your imagination to enrich your meditation? Return to the psalm you earlier read meditatively and reread it with an active imagination. Write down some of your thoughts.

Chapter Thirteen: Seeing Through Heaven's Eyes

* 1. How did the attitude of the saints of the past differ from their contemporaries, according to Bridget Herman?(see page 195). If you know someone with the same attitude, describe your experience with that person.

2. Write down reasons why we have trouble praying. Personalize the one that troubles you the most by writing out a prayer of confession expressing your feelings.

3. What does the author suggest as a reason for the greater ease with which women pray in public?(see page 198). If you are a married man, make this a journal entry about your attitudes and feelings about praying with your wife.

* 4. What is a sign of significant spiritual growth,
       according to the author? See page 199.

5. Make a journal entry describing your frustration
    with unanswered prayer.

6. What prayer is among the purest we can pray? See
    page 201.

7. Why does the author keep a prayer list?

8. Write out a prayer expression of adoration.

9.   If you were to confess to some of the sin "boulders"
      in your life, what would they be?

10.   What are the twelve "apostles of ill health,"
      according to E. Stanley Jones? (see pages 206 - 207).

* 11. If you were to visualize yourself as an intercessory
      prayer warrior, how would you describe your prayer
      life?

12.   What was the secret of the extraordinary leadership
      power of Eric Liddell, the missionary-prisoner? (see
      page 210).

13. Write out the deepest desire of your heart in respect to prayer.

Chapter Fourteen: Rest Beyond Leisure

1. What provided the "check and balance" in William Wilberforce's life in the face of "risings of ambition"? (see page 216).If you have had a similar experience, make a journal entry of it.

* 2. What is the paradox the author notes about our leisure society? See page 217.

* 3. How did God "close the loop" on His creation activity?

* 4. What is the foremost purpose for the rest instituted by God?

* 5. The author writes, "Work that goes on month after month without a genuine pause to inquire of its meaning and purpose may swell the bank account and enhance the professional reputation." What will it also do for all of us?

6. Are you experiencing the "rest that reaffirms truth"? If you are not, what steps do you need to take to make it happen?

7. What do you need to do to experience the kind of rest that redefines your mission in life?

* 8. What is the content of the Sabbath rest according to the author? See page 228.

9. What personal "Sabbath rest" plan could be possible for you and your spouse?

10. Make a journal entry of the key ideas/concepts you have absorbed from reading and studying this book. Then add some of the exciting developments as you have implemented recommended action.

Notes

Chapter 1

1. William Barclay, *The Letters to the Galatians and Ephesians* (Philadelphia: Westminster, 1976), p. 100.
2. Wayne Muller, *Sabbath: Finding Rest, Renewal, and Delight in Our Busy Lives* (New York: Bantam Doubleday Dell, 2000), p. 2.
3. Anne Morrow Lindbergh, *The Gift from the Sea* (New York: Pantheon, 1955), pp. 23-24.
4. Dorothie Bobbe, *Abigail Adams* (New York: Putnam, 1966), p. 206.

Chapter 2

1. *"Executive's Crisis,"* Wall Street Journal, 12 March 1982, p. 1.
2. James Buchan, *The Indomitable Mary Slessor* (New York: Seabury, 1981), p. 86.

Chapter 3

1. Cited in J. Oswald Sanders, *Spiritual Leadership* (Chicago: Moody, 1967), p. 23.

Chapter 4

1.   Paul Tournier, *Creative Suffering* (New York: Harper & Row, 1983).

Chapter 5

1.   Frank W. Boreham, *A Casket of Cameos* (1924: reprint, Valley Forge, PA: Judson, 1950), p. 266.
2.   Cardinal Danneels of Brussels, quoted in Jean Vanier, *Community and Growth* (Mahwah, NJ: Paulist Press), p. 210.
3.   Herbert Butterfield, *Christianity and History* (New York: Charles Scribner's Sons, 1949), p. 115.

Chapter 6

1.   William Barclay, *The Gospel of Matthew* (Philadelphia: Westminster, 1975), p. 280.

Chapter 7

1.   Elton Trueblood, *While It Is Day* (New York: Harper & Row, 1974), p. 67.
2.   Harold Begbie, *Life of General William Booth* (New York: MacMillan, 1920), p. 178.
3.   C. S. Lewis, *Letters to an American Lady* (Grand Rapids: Eerdmans, 1975), p. 53.

Chapter 8

1. David Denby, *Great Books* (New York: Simon & Schuster, 1997), p. 15.

2. Trueblood, *While It Is Day,* pp. 97-98.

3. E. Stanley Jones, *Song of Ascents* (Nashville: Abingdon, 1968), p. 189.

4. Norman Polmar and Thomas B. Allen, Rickover: *Controversy and Genius* (New York: Simon & Schuster, 1982), p. 267.

5. Harry A. Blamires, *The Christian Mind* (Ann Arbor: Servant, 1978).

6. Oswald Chambers, *Leagues of Light: Diary of Oswald Chambers 1915-1917* (Louisville, KY: Operation Appreciation Ministries), p. 42.

Chapter 9

1. Ernest Dimnet, *The Art of Thinking* (New York: Simon & Schuster, 1928).

Chapter 10

1. Howard Rutledge and Phyllis Rutledge with Mel White and Lyla White, *In the Presence of Mine Enemies* (Old Tappan, NY: Fleming Revell, 1973), p. 34.

2. Brother Lawrence, *The Practice of the Presence of God, trans. E. M. Blaiklock* (Nashville: Thomas Nelson, 1982).

3. Cited in Richard Foster, *Freedom of Simplicity* (New York: Harper & Row, 1981), p. 78.

Chapter 11

1. E. Stanley Jones, *The Divine Yes* (Nashville: Abingdon, 1975), p. 63.

2. Malcolm Muggeridge, *Something Beautiful for God* (Garden City, NY: Image, 1977), p. 48.

3. Henri J. M. Nouwen, *The Way of the Heart* (New York: Seabury, 1981), p. 39.

4. Wayne E. Oates, *Nurturing Silence in a Noisy Heart* (Garden City, NY: Doubleday, 1979), p. 3.

5. Paul Sangster, *Doctor Sangster* (New York: Epworth, 1962), p. 109.

6. Peter Alexander, *Alan Paton: A Biography* (Oxford University Press, 1994), p. 171.

Chapter 12

1. Jones, *Songs*, p. 104.

2. Clarence W. Hall, *Samuel Logan Brengle: Portrait of a Prophet* (Chicago: Salvation Army Supply & Purchasing Dept., 1933), p. 185.

3. John Baillie, *A Diary of Private Prayer* (New York: Charles Scribner's Sons, 1949), p. 27.

4. Lewis, *Letters*, p. 73.

Chapter 13

1. Bridget Herman, *Creative Prayer* (Cincinnati: Forward Movement, n.d.), p. 16.

2. Kelly, *A Testament of Devotion* (New York: Harper & Row, 1941), p. 39.

3. Lawrence, *Practice*, p. 70.

4. Henri J. M. Nouwen, *Clowning in Rome* (Garden City, NY: Image, 1979), p. 73.

5. Kelly, *Devotion*, p. 54.

6. Hall, *Portrait of a Prophet*, p. 237.

7. Jones, *Song*, p. 337.

8. Hall, *Portrait of a Prophet*, p. 185.

9. Sally Magnusson, *The Flying Scotsman* (New York: Quartet Books, 1981), p. 165.

Chapter 14

1. Garth Lean, *God's Politician* (London: Darton, Longman & Todd, 1980), p. 89.

2. Lawrence, *Practice*, p. 85.

3. Abraham Heschel, *The Earth Is the Lord's and The Sabbath* (two books published as one, New York: Harper Torchbooks, 1966), p. 10.

4. Hugh Evan Hopkins, *Charles Simeon of Cambridge* (Grand Rapids: Eerdmans, 1977), pp. 155-56.